LOVERS

by
BRIAN FRIEL

Part One — WINNERS

Part Two — LOSERS

D0660866

THE DRAMATIC PUBLISHING COMPANY

LOVERS was presented by Helen Bonfils and Morton Gottlieb at the Vivian Beaumont Theatre in New York as a part of the Lincoln Center Festival. It was held over for an extended run at the Music Box Theatre before going on tour. The playbill is reproduced below.

———— •—•—— ————

HELEN BONFILS AND MORTON GOTTLIEB

by arrangement with Oscar Lewenstein

present

ART CARNEY

in

LOVERS

A Play in Two Parts by
BRIAN FRIEL

The Edwards-MacLiammoir Dublin Gate Theatre Production

Directed by
HILTON EDWARDS

with

ANNA MANAHAN	**EAMON MORRISSEY**	**FIONNUALA FLANAGAN**
BEULAH GARRICK		**GRANIA O'MALLEY**

Scenery by **William Ritman**	Costumes by **Noel Taylor**	Lighting by **Tharon Musser**

———— •—•—— ————

Part One

WINNERS

Episode 1

(When the curtain rises, a MAN and a WOMAN are seated
on two high-backed chairs, one D L and one D R,
at the edge of the stage. They are the Commentators. They are in their late fifties and carefully dressed in good dark clothes. Each has a
book on his knee--not a volume, preferably a
bound manuscript--and they read from this every
so often. Their reading is impersonal, complete-
ly without emotion: their function is to give information. At no time must they reveal an attitude
toward their material.)

Between them and slightly upstage is Ardnageeha, the
hill that overlooks the town of Ballymore. A large
pentagonal platform, approached by four or five
shallow steps all around would be sufficient. This
is the only stage furniture.)

MAN.
At approximately 9:45 on the morning of Saturday,
June 4, 1966 Margaret Mary Enright set out from
her home, a detached red-brick house on the out-
skirts of the town of Ballymore, County Tyrone,
Northern Ireland.   Before she left she brought
breakfast to her mother who was still in bed; and
as she passed her father's surgery, which is built
as an annex to the house, she tapped with the back
of her fingers on the frosted glass panel of the
door. In a small attache case she has her schoolbooks and sandwiches for lunch.   She cycled
through the town and at High Street she met two
friends and stopped to talk to them: Joan O'Hara,
a classmate, and Philip Moran. They told her
they planned to go boating on Lough Gorm that
afternoon and asked her to join them. She said
perhaps she would. Then she cycled out the Mill

Road until she came to Whelan's Brae. There
she left the road and pushed her bicycle----

(MAG enters at this point. She is seventeen, bubbling
with life. Although she is not really very beautiful, her vivacity gives her a distinct attraction.)

MAN.
--across the fields until she came to the foot of
Ardnageeha, the hill that overlooks the town of
Ballymore. She left her bicycle at the bottom of
Ardnageeha, and climbed to the top. It was a
glorious summer's morning. Temperatures were
in the lower 70's. And there was no wind.
(When MAG gets to the top of the hill, she
looks around for Joe. He has not arrived
yet. She lights a cigarette, squats on the
ground, and waits for him.)

WOMAN.
At roughly the same time as Margaret Enright
set out, Joseph Michael Brennan left his home
at 37, Railway Terrace. His mother had gone
to work two hours previously and had left his
breakfast ready for him. His father was still in
bed and asleep. He went out through the back
yard, down the mews lane and across the waste
ground between the rear of Railway Terrace and
the railway line. On his way across the waste
ground he met some children who were throwing
stones at rats. He followed the line out past the
marshaling yard, under the iron bridge, and for
a mile out into the country. He carried his schoolbooks in a leather satchel. When he got to the
level-crossing he cut across the fields until he
came to the foot of Ardnageeha, the hill that overlooks the town of Ballymore.

(JOE enters here. He is seventeen and a half, a serious boy and a good student, interested in books.)

WOMAN.

> Then he climbed to the top.
>> (MAG sees him coming up the hill. She goes down the far side, i. e. up stage, until she is out of sight. There she hides.)

MAN.

> Margaret Enright was a pupil of St. Mary's Grammar School, run by the Sisters of Mercy. And Joseph Brennan was a pupil of St. Kevin's College, a grammar school for boys run by the clergy of the diocese. She was seventeen; he seventeen and a half. And they had their books with them because school was officially over for the year and they planned to spend the day study- ing for their final examinations at the end of their grammar school course. The examinations be- gan the following Wednesday.

JOE.

> Maggie! Maggie? (Shouts.) Maaaaaag!
>> (When he gets no response he squats on the ground, opens his bag, takes out a book, and begins to work.)

WOMAN. They stayed on top of Ardnageeha, that over- looks the town of Ballymore, from 10:00 until 2:00. They had their lunch up there. We can assume that they did some work because Joseph was an excellent student, not brilliant, but very keen and very industrious. Margaret was no scholar. She was intelligent but scattered. And we can assume that they talked some and perhaps dreamed some, because they were young and the day was beauti- ful. And even though the examinations were im- minent, they cannot have been all that important to the young pair who were to be married in exactly three weeks' time, on Saturday, June 25, because Margaret was pregnant.

> (JOE glances up from his work and scans the land below him. No sign of MAGGIE. He returns to his book. Now MAGGIE creeps up behind him and pounces on his back, trying to push him to the edge of the hill so that he will roll down. They wrestle for a few seconds.)

JOE.

Come on! Cut it out, will you! That'll do!

MAG.

Ha! You leaped like a rabbit!

JOE.

I was looking for you. Where were you?

MAG.

Waiting for you. You're late.

JOE.

I was here at ten exactly.

MAG.

I've been here for at least half an hour.
> (She throws herself on the ground in exaggerated exhaustion, produces cigarettes, and begins talking. During most of this episode JOE is studying, or trying to study. But occasionally he tunes in to her prattle. By throwing in an occasional word he gives her the impression he is conversing with her.)

JOE.

Did you walk it?

MAG.

> The bike's lying at the foot of the hill.

JOE.

> I didn't see it.

MAG.

> Sure, you're half-blind! God, my tongue's hang-
> ing out for a reek after that!
>> (Inhales and exhales with satisfaction.)
> Aaaah, bliss! Sister Pascal says: You may search
> the lists of the canonized but you will search in
> vain for the saint that smoked. Maybe you'll be
> a saint, Joe.

JOE.

> Let's get started.

MAG.

> I read in a book that there are 1, 200, 000 nuns in
> the world. Isn't that fierce? Imagine if they were
> all gathered in one place--on an island, say--
> and the Chinese navy was let loose at them--
> cripes, you'd hear the squeals in Tobermore!
> I have a wicked mind, too. D'you ever think things
> like that, Joe? I'm sure you don't. I think that
> women have far more corrupt minds than men,
> but I think that men are more easily corrupted
> than women.

JOE.

> We'll get a couple of hours done before we eat.

MAG (with excessive disgust).

> Food! I don't care if I never see another bite
> ever again. My God, I thought I was going to
> vomit my guts out this morning! And this could
> keep up for the next seven months, according to
> Doctor Watson. The only consolation is that

you're all right. It would be wild altogether if
you were at it, too. Sympathetic sickness, they
call it. But it's only husbands get it. Maybe you'll
get it this day three weeks--the minute we get
married--God, wouldn't that be a scream! D'you
know what Joan O'Hara told me? That all the
time her mother was expecting Oliver Plunket,
her father never lifted his head out of the kitchen
sink. Isn't it crazy! And for the last three days
he lay squealing on the floor like a stuck pig and
her mother had to get the police for him in the
end. I love this view of Ballymore: the town and
the fields and the lake; and the people. When I'm
up here and look down on them, I want to run
down and hug them all and kiss them. But then
when I'm down among them I feel like doing that--
      (She cocks a snook into Joe's face.)
--into their faces. I bet you that's how God feels
at times, too. Wouldn't you think so?

JOE.
      I don't know how God feels.

MAG.
      Why not?

JOE.
      Because I'm not God.

MAG.
      Oh, you're so clever! Well, I'll tell you some-
      thing: there are occasions in my life when I
      know how God feels.

JOE.
      Good for you.

MAG.
      And one of those occasions is now.

(Puffing her cigarette regally.)
At this moment God feels . . . expansive . . .
and beneficent . . . and philanthropy.

JOE.

Philanthropic.

MAG (after momentary setback).
And we will not be put into bad humor by grubby
little pedants.

JOE.

Look, Mag: we came up here to study. What
are you going to do first?

MAG.

French.   And then maths. And then Spanish.
And then English language and literature. And
after lunch geography and the history of the world.
I have planned a program for myself.   The important thing about revising for an examination
is to have a method. What are you starting with?

JOE.

Maths.

MAG.

Then what?

JOE.

That's all.

MAG.

Only maths?

JOE.

Huh-huh.
   (She considers this absurd idea for a second. Then, because JOE is wiser in these

things than she, she readily agrees with
him.)

MAG.

Then that's what I'll do, too.
(Really worries.)
My God, if the volume of a cone doesn't come
up, I'm scootrified! Not that I care--I can af-
ford to go down in one subject.
(Pause.)
Joe . . .

JOE.

What?

MAG.

What's the real difference between language and
literature?

JOE.

You're not serious, Maggie!

MAG.

Don't--don't--don't tell me . . . I remember
now . . . One is talking and the other is . . .
books!

JOE.

Talking? . . .

MAG.

That's it.

JOE.

That's no definition! Language is----

MAG.

Don't say another word. I have it in my head.
But if you start lecturing, I'll lose it again. I

have my own way of remembering things. Joe,
last night again Papa asked me to let him get
the flat painted for us before we move in.

JOE (doggedly).
I said I'll paint the flat.

MAG.
That's what I told him. And I was thinking,
Joe . . .

JOE.
What?

MAG.
If we put a lace curtain across the kitchen win-
dow we wouldn't actually see down into the slaugh-
terhouse yard.

JOE.
And if we wore ear-plugs all the time we
wouldn't actually hear the mooing and the
shooting.

MAG (softly to herself).
And even if a curtain did make the room darker,
it'll still be lovely.

JOE.
I signed the lease yesterday evening.

MAG (absolutely thrilled).
It's ours now? We own it?

JOE.
Old Kerrigan was so busy working he wouldn't
take time off to go into the office; so we put
the document on the back of a cow that was
about to be shot and that's where we signed

it. Cockeyed old miser!

MAG.

He's not!

JOE.

What?

MAG.

Cockeyed.

JOE.

I'm telling you. And crazy, too. In a big rubber
apron and him dripping with blood. And cows and
sheep and bullocks dropping dead all around him.

MAG.

Oh, God, my stomach!
(JOE realizes that his tale is successful.
He gets up on his feet to enact the scene.
MAG listens with delight and soon gets
drawn into the pantomime.)

JOE.

"Drive them up there! Another beast. Come on!
Come on! I haven't all day. And what's bother-
ing you, young Brennan? Steady, there! Steady!
Bang! Bang! Drag it away! Slit its throat! Slice
it open! Skin it!"

MAG.

Stop--stop!

JOE.

"Another beast! Get a move on! What am I paying you fellas for?" You told me to call about
that flat, Mr. Kerrigan. "Steady--bang! Bang!
Damnit, I nearly missed--bang!--that's it.
Drag him off. What are you saying, young

Brennan? The lease? Oh, the lease! Oh, aye,
Here we are.
>   (JOE produces an imaginary document
>   from his hip pocket.)

Best flat in town. Hell, it's all blood now.
>   (JOE wipes the imaginary document on
>   his leg.)

Come on! Another animal! There's a fine
beast for you, Brennan! Look at those shanks!
Bang! Bang! Never knew what hit him! I sign
here, son, don't I?
>   (JOE pretends to write; but the pen does
>   not work and he flings it away.)

Hell, that doesn't write. "

MAG.

> Bang! Bang!

JOE.

> "Keep behind me, young Brennan. This is a
> dangerous job. "

MAG.

> Let's sign it in blood, young Brennan.

JOE.

> Finest view in town. And the noise down here's
> great company. Bang! Bang!

MAG.

> Like living in Dead Man's Creek.

JOE.

> There's a bullock that looks like the president
> of St. Kevin's. Bang! Bang!

MAG.

> A sheep the image of Sister Paul. Bang! Bang!

JOE.
>   Drag 'em away!

MAG.
>   Slice 'em open!

JOE.
>   Joan O'Hara's white poodle, Tweeny.

MAG.
>   Bang! And Philip Moran's mother.

JOE.
>   Bang! Bang! Doctor Watson.

MAG.
>   A friend. Pass, friend, pass.

JOE.
>   Skinny Skeehan, the solicitor.

MAG.
>   Bang-bang-bang-bang! Look--reverend mother!

JOE.
>   Where ɾ

MAG.
>   To the right--behind the rocks!

JOE (calling sweetly).
>   Mother Dolores.

MAG (answering sweetly).
>   Yes, Joseph?

JOE (viciously).
>   Bang-bang-bang!
>   (MAG grabs her stomach and falls slowly.)

MAG.
> Into thy hands, O Lord----

JOE.
> Bang!
>> (The final bullet enters her shoulder.)

MAG.
> Oh, shite!
>> (MAG rolls on the ground, helpless with
>> laughter.)

JOE.
> The town clerk--bang! All the teachers--bang!

MAG.
> The church choir----

JOE.
> Bang! Everyone that lives along snobby, snotty
> Melville Road--bang-bang-bang-bang-bang!

MAG.
> A holy-cost, by God.
>> (JOE listens attentively. Silence.)

JOE.
> Everything's quiet. Now we'll have peace to
> study. Back to the books.

MAG.
> I'm sore all over. (Searching.) Give us a
> fag quick.

JOE (bashfully).
> I'm afraid--I--sort of--sort of lost my head
> there, ma'am.

MAG.
> Does your mother know you act the clown like

that?

JOE.

Does your father know you smoke? Look at
the time it is! I came here to work.
(He goes back to his books. He is im-
mediately immersed.)

MAG.

Joe . . .

JOE.

What?

MAG.

The flat's ours now?

JOE.

Isn't that what I'm telling you.

MAG.

You're sure you wouldn't like the top floor in
our house?

JOE.

Positive.

MAG (after moment's hesitation).
So am L I just wanted to know if you were, too.

JOE.

Good-by.

MAG.

It's only that Papa'll be lonely without me. For
his sake, really. But he'll get over that. And
it's just that this is the first time he'll ever have
been separated from me, even for a night. But
he'll get over it. All parents have to face it

sooner or later.
>(Happily.)
Besides, I can wheel the pram over every after-
noon.
>(She looks at JOE, lost in his books; and
>again she has the momentary dread of the
>exam.)
I'm like you, Joe. When I concentrate, you
could yell at me and I wouldn't hear you.
>(She opens a book--almost at random.
>Looks at the sky.)
It's going to be very warm . . .
>(She takes off her school blazer, rolls up
>the sleeves of her blouse, and stretches
>out under the sun.)
If we didn't have to work we could sun-bathe.
>(Pause.)
The Easter we were in Florence, I kept thinking about your father and how good the sun there
would have been for his asthma. I read in a book
that asthma is purely psychosomatic and that a
man with asthma has a mother-fixation. Crazy
the things they dig up, too. I'm glad Papa's not
a doctor or he'd be watching me for symptoms
all the time. Your parents are such wonderful
people, Joe. I'm crazy about them. And I'm
going to model myself on your mother. And
from now on I'm going to treat my own parents
with . . . with a certain dignity. My God, the
things they said to me--they seared my soul
forever----
>(And without drawing a breath she hums a
>few bars of a popular song. She has a book
>before her eyes--but her eyes are closed.)

MAN.

>Joseph Brennan was the only child of Mick and ›
>Nora Brennan. Because of his asthma, Mick
>Brennan has not had a job for over twenty years.

He receives unemployment benefit and this is
supplemented by the earnings of his wife who
works as a charwoman from 8:00 a. m. until
8:00 p. m., six days a week, for 2/6d an hour.
In a good week her wages come to around
£9/0/0d. She has £113/10/6d in post-office
savings and £3/5/7d in an ornate tea-caddy in
the kitchen. She is a quiet woman, and all her
dreams and love and hope and delight were
centered unashamedly in Joe. Mick Brennan--
or Mick the Moocher, as he is known in Bally-
more--is keenly interested in horses, grey-
hounds, ferrets, and pigeons. He spends most
of his day at the greyhound-track. To his
friends he talked a lot about Joe, always re-
ferring to him in a casual, disparaging way as
The Lad. Nora Brennan has no hobbies.

WOMAN

Margaret Enright was the daughter of Walter
and Beth Enright. Walter is a dentist. When he
married he was the only dentist in Ballymore.
Now there are three; and his practice is the
smallest. As a young man he was interested in
books and travel and music. Now, after his
work, he sits at home, and drinks, and reads
thrillers. Beth, his wife, has been under
Doctor Watson's care for seventeen years, ever
since the death of her infant son. She gave birth
to twins -- Margaret and Peter -- and five days
after the birth Peter was discovered in his cot,
smothered by a pillow. She never fully recovered from this. In her good days she is
carefree -- almost reckless. In her bad days
she wears dark glasses and lies in bed. Walter
looks after her constantly.

(MAG is drowsy with the heat. Her head is
propped against her case. Through slitted
eyes she surveys the scene below in Ballymore. She is addressing JOE but knows that

he is not listening.)

MAG.

I can see the boarders out on the tennis courts.
They should be studying. And there's a funeral
going up High Street; nine cars, and a petrol
lorry, and an ambulance. Maybe the deceased
was run over by the petrol lorry--the father of
a large family--and the driver is paying his respects and crying his eyes out. If he doesn't stop
blubbering he'll run over someone else. And the
widow is in the ambulance, all in plaster, crippled
for life.

(She tries out a mime of this--both arms and
legs cast in awkward shapes.)

And the children are going to be farmed out to
cruel aunts with squints and mustaches. Sister
Michael has a beard. Joan O'Hara says she shaves
with a cut-throat every first Friday and uses
an after-shave called Virility. God, nuns are
screams if you don't take them seriously. I think
I'd rather be a widow than a widower; but I'd
rather be a bachelor than a spinster. And I'd
rather be deaf than dumb; but I'd rather be dumb
than blind. And if I had to choose between lung
cancer, a coronary, and multiple sclerosis, I'd
take the coronary. Papa's family all died of cor-
onaries, long before they were commonplace.

(She sits up to tell the following family history.)

He had a sister, Nan, who used to sing at the
parochial concert every Chrisimas; and one year,
when she was singing Jerusalem--you know just
before the chorus, when the piano is panting huh-
huh-huh-huh-huh-huh--she opened her mouth and
dropped like a log . . . Joe, d'you think--

(Quoting from something she has read.)

--my legs have got thick, my body gross, my
facial expression passive to dull, and my eyes

lack-luster? I hope it's a boy, and that it'll be like you--with a great big bursting brain. Or maybe it'll be twins--like me. I wonder what Peter would have been like. Sometimes when she's very ill Mother calls me Peter. If it were going to be twins I'd rather have a boy and a girl than two boys or two girls; but if it were going to be triplets I'd rather have two boys and a girl or two girls and a boy than three boys or three girls.
(Very wisely and directed to JOE.)
And I have a feeling it's going to be premature.
(JOE is alerted. His eyes move away from his book but his head does not move.)
Mothers have intuitions about these things. We were premature. Five weeks. Very tricky.

JOE.

Tricky?

MAG。

Caesarean, as a matter of fact.
(JOE has never heard the term.)

JOE (too casually).

That--sure--sure that's--so was I, too.

MAC (delighted).

Were you? Isn't that marvelous? We really have everything in common! Oh, Joe, wait till you hear; I was doing my hair this morning, and d'you know what I found in the comb? A gray hair! I'm old! Two months pregnant and I'm as gray as a badger! Isn't it a scream! I think a young face and silver hair is more attractive than an old face and black hair. But if I had to choose between a young face and black hair and an old face and silver hair I think I'd prefer the young face.
(Gently.)

You have a young face. You're only a boy. You're
a baby, really. I'll have two babies to take care
of.
    (She touches his shoe.)
Joe, we'll be happy, Joe, won't we? It's such
a beautiful morning. So still; I think this is the
most important moment in my life. And I think--
    (She laughs with embarrassment.)
--I think sometimes that happiness, real happiness, was never discovered until we discovered
it. Isn't that silly? And I want to share it with
everyone--everywhere.

JOE.

    Stupid.

MAG.

    What?

JOE.

    A fat lot you have to give.

MAG.

    I didn't say give!

JOE.

    You did!

MAG.

    I did not!

JOE.

    I heard you!

MAG.

    Liar! I said "share"!

JOE.

    Share what?

MAG.

>You wouldn't understand!

JOE.

>Understand what?
>>(MAG has lost the thread of the argument.)

MAG.

>Anything! 'Cause you're just a selfish, cold,
>horrible, priggish, conceited donkey! Stuck
>in your old books as if they were the most im-
>portant thing in the world; and your--your--
>your intended waiting like a dog for you to toss
>her a kind word!

JOE.

>I only asked----

MAG.

>You hate me--that's it--you're going to marry
>me just to crush me! I've heard of men like you
>--sadicists! I've read about them in books! But
>I never thought for a second----
>>(She breaks off suddenly and clasps her
>>stomach in terrified agony. At the same
>>time she is pleasantly aware of Joe's
>>mounting panic.)
>Oh, my God!

JOE.

>What?

MAG.

>Oooooooooh!

JOE.

>What--what--what is it, Maggie?

MAG.

>Joe!

JOE.
> Mag, are you sick? Are you sick, Mag?

MAG (formally).
> Labor has commenced.

JOE (in panic).
> Sweet God! How d'you know? What's happening?
> I'll get help! Don't move! Dr. Watson warned you
> to stop cycling! How d'you feel? I'll carry you.
> Don't move--don't move!
>> (In total consternation he searches her face,
>> noting every flicker of every feature. She is
>> gratified at his anxiety. She acts the brave
>> sufferer.)

MAG.
> I . . . think----

JOE.
> Don't talk! Don't move! Where did you leave
> your bike?

MAG.
> Stay with me, Joe, please. Hold my hand.

JOE.
> God, this is fierce! On top of a bloody hill!
> You're all right, Mag, aren't you? Aren't
> you all right?
>> (She gives him a brave smile.)

MAG.
> Dear Joe, I'm fine, thank you, Joe.

JOE.
> What's happening? Tell me.

MAG.
> Nothing to be alarmed about. False pains.

JOE.

 False? . . .

MAG (cheerily).
 Gone again. For the time being.

JOE.
 They'll be back?

MAG.
 Oh, yes. But maybe not for a month.

JOE.
 God, I'm not worth tuppence.

MAG.
 I'm sorry for calling you names.

JOE.
 Maybe you should go home, Mag, eh?

MAG.
 I'm fine. Really. Go on with your work.

JOE.
 God, I don't know.

MAG (smiling reassuringly).
 Please. I'll just rest.
  (JOE gropes for something tender to
  say. But he is too embarrassed.)

JOE.
 Maggie, I'll . . . I'll try . . . I'll try to be----

MAG (a revelation).
 I know now!

JOE.
 Huh?

MAG.

> No breakfast!

JOE.

> What are you----

MAG.

> Hunger pangs! That's what it was! I'm ravenous!

JOE.

> Hunger? . . .

MAG.

> I could eat the side of a horse!

JOE.

> But you said you didn't care----

MAG.

> Don't be always quoting what I said. There's nothing as detestable as being quoted. I change my mind every two minutes. Or would you rather it was labor?

JOE (totally baffled).

> I . . . I . . .
>> (Resolutely.)
> I'm going to work.
>> (He begins to study again. MAG opens her case and takes out a packet of sandwiches.)

MAG.

> All the same, if I eat now, I'll have nothing left for later. I'll do with two small sandwiches. Three.
>> (Eats vigorously.)
> My big regret now is that I dropped domestic science in junior. Can't even remember how

to make rock buns. And poor old Dorothy Quilty
was so sweet to us all. Did I ever tell you what
happened to her, Joe?

> (She waits for a reply, gets none, and goes
> on anyhow.)

She was from Dublin. And one afternoon, during
the Christmas holidays, she went to the pictures.
And this man sat in the seat beside her--gospel
truth--Joan O'Hara heard it from a cousin of hers
who's a guard in Dundalk. And anyhow during
the film, this fellow gave her an injection in the
arm. Of course no one saw him. And when she
passed out he carried her out to the street, and
his accomplice was waiting there in a car, and
they drove off with her.

> (Waits again for Joe's reaction. Then goes
> on.)

And four days later she was found in the Wicklow
mountains--up a sycamore tree.

> (JOE turns around slowly to face her.)

JOE.
> What d'you mean--up a sycamore tree?

MAG.
> Hiding.

JOE.
> Hiding what?

MAG.
> Herself. In the leaves.

JOE (deliberately).
> You really are crazy.

MAG.
> She was hiding in the leaves, stupid, because
> they had taken her clothes away--that's the way.

And for your knowledge and information she had
to give up teaching after that experience. Nervous . . . Nervosity; that's what the doctor said
she had. And she's now a stitcher in a Belfast
shirt factory--of all girls.

JOE.

For a woman that's going to be married in four
weeks' time----

MAG.

Three.

JOE.

--honest to God, the stories that you come out
with--juvenile, that's the only word for them.
And I'm trying to work at integration. So will
you shut up?

MAG (with dignity).

I will. I certainly will. And the next time I
break breath with you, you'll be a chastened
man.
(Brief pause.)
But before I go silent for the rest of the day,
there's something I want to get clear between
us, Joseph Brennan.
(Pause.)
Joe.

JOE.

What?

MAG.

You never proposed to me.

JOE.

Huh?

MAG.

>You haven't <u>asked</u> me to marry you.

JOE.

>What are you raving about?

MAG.

>Propose to me.

JOE.

>God!

MAG.

>Now.

JOE.

>You really are----

MAG.

>Ask me.

JOE.

>Will-you-marry-me. Now!

MAG.

>Thank you, Joseph. I will.
>>(He goes back to his books.)

JOE.

>Bats! Raving bloody bats!

MAG.

>The children will want to know. Especially the
>girls. And I'll tell them it was a beautiful morn-
>ing in June, a Saturday, four days before the ex-
>ams began, on top of Ardnageeha, the Hill of the
>Wind. And everything was still. And their fath-
>er said, "Maggie," very shyly, "Maggie Enright,
>will you make me the proudest and happiest man

in the whole world? Will you be my spouse?" And
I said, "Joe"--nothing more. And I think that
was the most important moment in my life.
>   (She looks at JOE, sees him engrossed in
>   his work, has a sudden stab of anxiety, and
>   grabs a book.)
I really am scootrified this time! Integration--
that's on my course, too--I think. What in the
name of God does it mean?
>   (She buries her head in her hands and studies
>   furiously.)

MAN.

It is estimated that Joe Brennan and Maggie Enright came down from the top of Ardnageeha
around two o'clock that afternoon. They were
seen walking hand-in-hand along the Mill Road
at about ten past two; and ten minutes later they
were seen going in the direction of Lough Gorm,
which lies to the east of Ballymore. Both were
on foot. Joe was wheeling Maggie's bicycle. The
recorded temperature at 3:00 p.m. on that Saturday afternoon, June 4, 1966 was 77 degrees. And
there was no wind.

WOMAN.

Lough Gorm is three miles long and half a mile
broad, and there are forty-nine islands of various sizes scattered over it. There are seven
boats on the lake. And on that afternoon two of
them were out. Philip Moran and Joan O'Hara
were out in Mr. O'Hara's boat. They went out at
noon and returned at one-thirty. The other boat
was William Anthony Clerkin's, an accountant in
the local bank. He fished from eleven that morning until two that afternoon. Then he pulled in
on the south shore, beside the old lime kiln, and
went home for his lunch. He left the oars and
rowlocks lying in the boat. When he returned an

hour and twenty minutes later the boat was gone; and a girl's bicycle was lying at the edge of the water.

MAG.

I'll tell you a tip.
> (Pause.)

Joe.
> (Pause.)

D'you want to know a clever trick I have, Joe? In all exams the smart thing to do is to write down everything you know--no matter what the question is. *Les oyseaux qui en sont dehors désespèrent d'y entrer; et d'un pareil soing en sortir, ceulx qui sont au dedans;* if the moving line is at right angles to the plane figure, the prism is a right prism; in 1585 Sir Philip Sydney met his death at Zutphen from a wound in the nether regions of his body; the volume of a cone is 1/3 dh multiplied by--my God, and that's the one thing I know! Shakespeare, the Bard of Avon, besides writing thirty-four extant plays, was married to a woman eight years his senior, and was the father of twins. Like Papa. As flies to wanton boys are we to the gods; they kill us for their sport. Sister Pascal says that you always know Protestants by their yellow faces and Catholics by their dirty fingernails.

> (She rises, moves away from JOE, who is lost in his books, and stands at the edge of the hill-top. She looks down over the town.)

Nuns are screams--if you don't take them seriously . . . I don't know what things I take seriously . . . Never books or school or things like that . . . Maybe God sometimes, when I'm in trouble . . . and Papa. . . . and being a good wife to you . . . It's so quiet, with the whole world before me . . . Joe--

> (She turns to face him.)

Joe, you'll have to talk a lot more to me, Joe. I don't care if it's not sensible talk; it's just that-- you know--I feel lonely at times . . . Of course I'll have Joan; she'll visit us; Phil and herself. And you'll like her better when you get to know her. All that's wrong with her is that she's not mature yet; and she can be cruel at times. . . . After we're married we'll have lots of laughs together, Joe, won't we? We'll laugh a lot, won't we?

(She begins to cry inaudibly.)

Joe, I'm nervous; I'm frightened, Joe; I'm terrified . . .

MAN.

At 6:20 William Anthony Clerkin reported to Sergeant Finlay that his boat had been stolen. The Sergeant and Mr. Clerkin returned to Lough Gorm and walked around a portion of the south shore. They sighted the upturned boat floating about fifty yards west of the biggest island, Oilean Na Gcrann.

WOMAN.

As a result of inquiries the Sergeant learned that the bicycle belonged to Margaret Mary Enright. He 'phoned the Enright home and discovered that the girl had left there early in the morning. He then called at the Brennan home and Mr. Brennan informed him that he had not seen his son all day.

MAG.

I will tell my secrets to my baby.

MAN.

It was then 7:45 p. m.

WOMAN.

At 8:10 a search party of twenty-three local men set out to search the forty-nine islands.

(MAG has another twinge of conscience; she
plunges into her book again.)

MAG (reading).

LP, MQ and NR are ordinates perpendicular to
the axis OX such that LP =8", MQ = 7", and NR =
4". Find the lengths of the ordinates at the mid-
points of LM and MN of the circular arc through
P, Q, and R, and by means of Simpson's Rule
and the five ordinates estimate . . .

(Her concentration fails.)

Everything's so still. That's what I love. At a
time like this, if I close my eyes and scarcely
breathe, I sometimes have very important philo-
sophic thoughts--about existence and life and et
cetera. That's what people mean when they talk
of a woman's intuitions. Every woman has intuitions, but I think that pregnant women have more
important intuitions than non-pregnant women.
And another thing, too: a woman's intuitions are
more important while she's pregnant than after
she's had her baby. So when you see a pregnant
woman sitting at the fire, knitting, not talking,
you can be sure she's having very important phil-
osophic thoughts about things. I wish to God I
could knit. Years and years ago in primary school
I began a pair of gloves; but the fingers scootrified
me and I turned them into ankle socks . . . I
think your father's a highly intellectual man, really, a born naturalist. And your mother--she's
so practical and so unassuming. That's what I
want to be. One of these days I'm going to stop
talking altogether--for good--and people will say:
Didn't Mrs. Joseph Brennan become dignified all
of a sudden? Since the baby arrived, I suppose.
I think now, Joe, it's going to be nineteen days
overdue. And in desperation they'll bring me into the hospital and put me on the treadmill--that's
a new yoke they have to bring on labor. Joan told

me about it. An aunt of a second cousin of hers
was on it non-stop for thirteen hours. They keep
you climbing up this big wheel that keeps giving
away under you. Just like the slaves in olden
times. And after the baby's born they'll keep it
in an oxygen tent for a fortnight. And when we
get it home it'll have to be fed with an eye-dropper
every forty-nine minutes and we'll get no sleep
at all and--

> (Sudden alarming thought.)

--my God, you won't get asthma like your father
when you get old, will you?

JOE.

> . . . equals 2.8 x t x p all over pv to the power
> of 1.4 x v . . .

MAG.

> Even if you do I'll rub your chest with menthol
> and give you the kiss of life.

JOE.

> Shhhhhh.
>
> (She watches him for a moment in silence.
> He is unaware of her existence.)

MAG.

> There's something I want to tell you, Joe, and
> there's something I want to ask you as well.
> And I think I'll ask you the thing I want to ask you
> before I tell you the thing I want to tell you.
>
> (Pause.)
>
> Joe.

JOE (very irritable).
> What-what-what?

MAG.

> My parents sleep in separate rooms. Do yours?

JOE.

> In our house there are two bedrooms. I'm in one of them.

MAG.

> And do they--have they a single bed or a double bed?

JOE.

> Double. Satisfied, nosey?

MAG (fully gratified).

> I knew that was a real marriage. That's what I want. Like your parents. Joe, there's something I want to try to explain to you, too.

JOE.

> Look--five minutes more--that's all I ask.
>   (He does not listen to her.)

MAG.

> I look at Papa and Mother, and Mr. and Mrs. O'Hara, and all the other parents and I think--I think--none of them knows what being in love really is. And that's why I think we're different. God, doesn't that sound stupid when you say it! But that's the way I feel, Joe. At this moment--here--now--I'm crazy about you--and mad and reckless, so that I want to shout to the whole town: I love Joe Brennan! I'm mad about him! I'd do anything for him! D'you hear me, Mother Dolores? I love him so much--so much--that I want to--to become him! Isn't that stupid? And when I look around me--at Papa and Mother and the O'Haras--I think: my God we'll never become like that because--don't laugh at me, Joe--because I think we're unique! Is that how you feel, too?
>   (JOE flings his book from him in exasperation. Speaks very articulately.)

JOE.

> You-are-a-bloody-pain-in-the-neck!
>> (Quickly.)
> You haven't shut up for five consecutive minutes
> since we got here! You have done no work your-
> self and you have wasted my morning, too! And
> if anyone should be working, it's you, because
> you haven't a clue about anything! In fact you're
> the stupidest person I ever met!

MAG.

> Stewbag!

JOE.

> Sticks and stones--go ahead!

MAG.

> And you can't kick a football the length of your-
> self!

JOE.

> What has that got to do with it?

MAG.

> That's what everybody calls you 'cause that's all
> you can do is stew--stew--stew!

JOE.

> Born stupid.

MAG (crying).
> Stewbag! Stewbag!

JOE.

> Bawl away. Bawl you head off. But if you think
> I'm going to waste my life in Skinny Skeehan's
> smelly office, that's where you're mistaken. You
> trapped me into marrying you--that's all right--
> I'll marry you. But I'll lead my own life. And

somehow--somehow I'll get a degree and be a maths teacher. And nobody, neither you nor your precious baby nor anyone else, is going to stop me! So put that in your pipe and smoke it!

(He opens his book and pretends to work, but he is too agitated. MAG covers her face and cries.)

MAN.

The search was continued without interruption for three days. An S. O. S. was broadcast, and ports and airports were watched. It was reported to the police that a young couple answering to the description were seen in Liverpool and later in the Waterford area. But an investigation proved both reports to be false. Margaret Mary Enright and Joseph Michael Brennan had disappeared.

WOMAN.

On Wednesday, June 8, the search was called off.

CURTAIN

Episode 2

(The sun is warmer because it is early afternoon. JOE
and MAG have had their lunch; papers and paper
cups are lying around. MAG is stretched out on
the ground, her head pillowed on her case, the
essence of sloth. Her eyes are closed. JOE is
working at a calculation with total concentration.)

WOMAN.
The months of June and July, 1966 were the warm-
est and driest Ballymore has had since records
have been kept. The water supply to the town had
to be cut off for three hours each morning because
the level of Lough Gorm dropped by almost two
feet.

MAN.
Beth Enright, Margaret's mother, spent the great-
er portion of these months in the County Psychi-
atric Clinic. She was visited daily by Walter, her
husband, and on two occasions by Nora Brennan,
Joseph's mother, who brought her grapes and
magazines.
(JOE has finished his calculation. He closes
his books with a satisfied flourish.)

JOE.
Maths done! They can do their damndest now--
I'm ready for them! I'll tell you something, Mag,
you know when you're sitting in the exam hall and
the papers have just been given out and your eye
runs down the questions? Well, those are the
happiest moments in my life. There's always that
tiny uncertainty that maybe this time they'll come
up with something that's going to throw you; but
that only adds to the thrill because you know in
your heart you're . . . invincible.

41

(He begins to put his books away; because he
is on top of his work he is in an expansive
mood.)

I didn't tell you, I met old Skinny Skeehan. "I'll
start you in my office, lad, as soon as your exams are over. On your mother's account I hope
you're a good time-keeper and that your writing
is legible." I never looked at him right before;
his eyelids are purple and his ears are all hairy.
So I just said to him, "Stick your clerkship up
your legal ass and get a lawnmower at those ears
of yours"--like hell. But that's what I should have
said, the hungry get.

(Mentally ticking off.)

Another hour to French and the same at history
and I'll leave the English to tomorrow. Remember I was telling you how George Simpson got an
extern degree at London University? Well, I
wrote to them last night for a syllabus. Three
years, that's all it takes. Joseph Brennan, Bachelor of Science. Then, by God, the world's our
oyster. You asleep, Mag?

(MAG neither moves nor opens her eyes.)

MAG.

No.

JOE.

Nothing wrong with you, is there?

MAG.

No.

JOE.

Are you in bad form or something?

MAG.

No.

JOE.

Did I do anything, Mag?

MAG.

No.

JOE.

As long as those false pains don't come back.
    (Going on gaily.)
Pity we hadn't our togs. Be a great day for a
swim, wouldn't it?

MAG.

I trapped you into marrying me--that's what
you said.

JOE.

Huh?

MAG.

That's what you said--Put that in your pipe and
smoke it--that's what you said.

JOE.

Ah, come on, Mag. You're not huffing still.

MAG.

And you meant it, too.

JOE.

But you ate your lunch and all. You ate more
than I did.

MAG.

There was hate in your eyes.

JOE.

I'm sorry.

MAG.

>It's no good.
>>(Pause. Then JOE decides to win her around by clowning.)

JOE.

>Mag----

MAG.

>I'm not looking.

JOE.

>Mag----

MAG.

>No。

JOE.

>Who's this, Mag?

MAG.

>I'm going asleep.

JOE (in mincing voice).

>"Tweeny--Tweeny--Tweeny--Tweeny! Come on, Tweeny girl. Atta girl. Come on. Come on."

MAG.

>That's not one bit like Mr. O'Hara.

JOE (in excessive nasal tones).

>"Good example is something we should all practice, my dear people. Put one bad apple into a barrel of good apples, and all the good apples become corrupt."

MAG.

>I'm not listening.

JOE.

"But put one good apple into a barrel of bad apples, and then--and then----"

MAG.

You're not one bit funny.

JOE.

"--and then--
(Rapidly.)
--devotions this evening at six o'clock in the name of the Father Son Holy Ghost."

MAG (in matching tone).
Ha-men.

JOE (East London).

"So sorry, Joseph, but my Phil 'e's not at 'ome at present."
(MAG suddenly giggles.)
" 'E's out on 'is bi-cycle on one of 'is solitary nature rambles."
(MAG sits up. She laughs out loud.)
"Like 'is poor dad used to. I'll tell 'im you called. Bye-bye."

MAG.

"Ta-ta."

JOE.

"Ta-ta."

MAG.

No-- "Ta-ta for now."

JOE.

"Ta-ta for now."

MAG.
>"Call again soon, Joseph."

JOE.
>"I like my Phil to 'ave chum boys."
>>(They both howl with spontaneous, helpless laughter. When they try to speak they cannot finish.)

MAG.
>Sister Pascal----

JOE.
>Wha----

MAG.
>Sister Pascal----

JOE.
>--is a rascal!

MAG.
>She says that for every five minutes you laugh, you----

JOE.
>You what?

MAG.
>--you cry for ten!
>>(This seems the crowning absurdity. They roll on the ground.)

JOE.
>Oooooooh . . . !

MAG.
>God, I'm sore!

JOE.

Cruel!

MAG.

We'll cry for weeks!

JOE.

Nuns--bloody nuts!

MAG.

Give me a handkerchief.
(He throws her one. She wipes her eyes.
They sober up--and wonder what set them
off. She lights a cigarette.)

JOE.

What started that?

MAG.

I don't know.

JOE.

Give me (handkerchief). Oh, my God.

MAG.

Leave you weak.

JOE.

This whole town's nuts.
(MAG is stretched out under the sun again.
A wistful mood creeps over them now that
the laughter is forgotten.)

MAG.

D'you think they'll get married?

JOE.

Who?

MAG.
>Joan and Philip.

JOE.
>How would I know. They're only seventeen.

MAG.
>They say they're both going to be architects.

JOE.
>How long does that take?

MAG.
>Seven years. Maybe then.
>>(JOE busies himself with gathering up the
>>remains of the lunch.)

JOE.
>Maybe then what?

MAG.
>Maybe then they'll marry, after they qualify.

JOE.
>Maybe. Who cares?

MAG.
>I don't.

JOE.
>Neither do I.

MAG.
>Why talk about them then?

JOE.
>You mentioned them first.

MAG.
>You did. You imitated Mr. O'Hara and Phil's

mother.

JOE.

> Maggie, I did not mention Joan O'Hara's name.
> As a matter of fact, I can't stick that girl.

MAG.

> Sister Pascal was right.

JOE.

> What about?

MAG.

> We <u>will</u> cry for twice the length.

JOE.

> For God's sake, woman!
> > (He heads off down the far side of the hill to
> > get rid of the old papers he has gathered.)

MAG (quickly).

> Where are you going?

JOE.

> I am going to dispose of this stuff--if I have your
> permission.

MAG.

> You don't have to have my permission for any-
> thing. And I don't have to have yours, either.
> 'Cause I'm not married to you yet, Mr. Bren-
> nan, in case you have forgotten.

JOE.

> No, I haven't forgotten.
> > (He disappears. She calls after him.)

MAG.

> Well, just in case you should!

(She settles back and closes her eyes reso-
lutely.)

MAN.

On Tuesday, June 21, a local boy was driving his
father's cows down to the edge of Lough Gorm for
a drink when he saw what he described as "bundles of clothes" floating just off the north shore.
He ran home and told his mother.

WOMAN.

The police were informed, and Sergeant Finlay
accompanied by two constables went to investigate.
The "bundles" were the bodies of Margaret Mary
Enright and Joseph Michael Brennan. They were
floating, fully clothed, face down, in twenty-seven
inches of water.

MAN.

A post-mortem was held in the parochial hall at
7:00 p.m. that evening.
        (JOE has returned. He speaks with a digni-
        fied sincerity.)

JOE.

Mag, there is something I never told you. And
since you are going to be my wife, I don't want
there to be any secrets between us. I have a post-
office book. I have had it since I was ten. And
there is £23/15/0d. in it now. I intend spending
that money on a new suit, new shoes, and an elec-
tric razor. And I'm mentioning this to you now in
case you suspect I have other hidden resources.
I haven't.
        (He cannot maintain this tone. He continues
        naturally.)
And I was working out our finances. The rent of
the flat's two-ten. That'll leave us with about
four-ten. And if I could get some private pupils,

that would bring in another--say--thirty bob. We can manage fine on that, can't we? I mean, I can. What about you?

(Looks down at her.)

Mag? You asleep, Mag? How the hell can you sleep when you have no work done! Maggie? . . .

(He kneels beside her and looks into her face. He gently puts her hair away from her eyes. He straightens up as he remembers the word Caesarean.)

Dictionary . . .

(He gets his own dictionary and searches for the word.)

Cadet . . . cadge . . . Caesar . . . Caesarean, pertaining to Caesar or the Caesars--section-- an operation by which the walls of the stomach are cut open and . . .

(Shocked and frightened.)

. . . Cripes!

(Reads.)

--as with Julius--oh, my God! If I see you on that bike again I'll break your bloody neck! As with Julius--good God! Maggie, are you all right, Maggie? Oh, God, that's wild, wild! Sleep, Mag, that's bound to be good for you.

(He lifts her blazer and spreads it over her.)

There. God almighty! Cut open.

(Takes the blazer off.)

Maybe you'll be too warm. God, I'd sit ten exams every day sooner than this! Don't say a word, Maggie; just sleep and rest! That twenty-three pound fifteen--it's for you, Maggie. And I want you to--to--to squander it just as you wish: fur coats, dresses, perfumes, make-up, all that stuff--anything in the world you want--don't even tell me what you spend it on; I don't want to know. It's yours. And curtains for the window--whatever you like. God, Mag, I never thought for a minute it was that sort of thing!

(He looks closely at her.)

Mag . . .

(Whispers.)

Mag, I'm not half good enough for you. I'm jealous and mean and spiteful and cruel. But I'll try to be tender to you and good to you; and that won't be hard because even when I'm not with you--just when I think of you--I go all sort of silly and I say to myself over and over again: I'm crazy about Maggie Enright; and so I am--crazy about you. You're a thousand times too good for me. But I'll try to be good to you; honest to God, I'll try.

(He kisses her hand and replaces it carefully across her body. Then with sudden venom.)

Those Caesars were all gets!

(He takes an apple from one of the lunch bags, gets out his penknife, and peels it. As he does he talks to MAG even though he knows she is asleep.)

I hope it's a girl, like you; with blonde hair like yours. 'Cause if it's a boy it'll be a bloody hash, like me. And every night when I come home from Skeehan's office I'll teach her maths and she'll grow up to be a prodigy. I saw a program on TV once about an American professor who spoke to his year-old daughter in her cot in four different languages for an hour every day; and when the child began to talk she could converse in German, French, Spanish and Italian. Imagine if my aul fella looked down into our wee girl's cot and she shouted up to him *"Buenos dias!"* Cripes, he'd think she was giving him a tip for a horse! I hope to God it's a girl. But if it's twins I'd rather have two boys or two girls than . . .

(He glances shyly at MAGGIE and trails off sheepishly when he realizes he has fallen into her speech pattern.)

. . . D'you hear me? That's the way married people go. They even begin to look alike. Wonder,

is old Skinny Skeehan married? I bet she looks
like a gate-post. . . . Your father, Mag, my
God, he's such a fine man. And your mother--
I mean she's such a fine woman. I remember--
oh, I was only a boy at the time--I remember see-
ing them walking together out the Dublin Road;
And I thought they were so--you know--so dignified looking. I'd like to be like him. God, such
a fine man. And so friendly to everyone. You're
lucky to have parents like that. . . . My aul fella
--lifting the dole on a Friday--that's what he lives
for. She laughs and calls him her man Friday;
but I don't know how she can laugh at it. And to
listen to him talking--cripes, you'd think he was
bloody Solomon. How he can sit on his backside
and watch her go out every morning with her apron
wrapped in a newspaper under her arm--- Honest to God, I don't know how he does it. I said it
to her once, you know; called him a loafer or
something. And you should have seen her face!
I thought she was going to hit me! "Don't you ever
--ever--say the likes of that again. You'll never
be half the man he is. " Loyalty, I suppose; 'cause
when you're that age, you hardly--you know--
really love your husband or wife any more. . . .
Did I ever tell you what he does when there's no
racing? He has this tin trunk under his bed; he
keeps all my old school reports in it. And he sits
up there in the cold and takes out the trunk and
pores over all those old papers--term reports
and all, away back to my primary school days!
Real nut! I know damn well when he's at it 'cause
I can hear the noise of the trunk on the lino. And
once when I went into the room he tried to stuff
all the papers out of sight. Strange, too, isn't
it . . . You know, we never speak at all, except
maybe "Is the tea ready?" or "Bring in some
coal. " . . . Sitting up there in that freezing at-
tic, going over my old marks . . . Maybe when

I'm older, maybe we'll go to football matches
together, like Peadar Donnelly and his aul fella . . . I don't like football matches but he
does; and we wouldn't have to speak to each
other -- except going and coming back . . . .
Three years is no length for a degree. And I
think myself I'd be a good teacher.
>   (MAG speaks but does not move or open
>   her eyes. Her voice is sleepy.)

MAG.
>   What time is it?

JOE.
>   Quarter to two.

MAG.
>   Call me at half-past, will you? I have a bit of
>   revision to do.

JOE.
>   A bit! You've done nothing!
>>   (MAG has dropped off again.)
>   Mag!

MAG.
>   Mm?

JOE.
>   That's all right! You go ahead and sleep! But
>   I'm telling you; if I die of a heart attack and
>   leave you with a dozen kids, you'll be damned
>   sorry you haven't your G. C. E. ordinary levels!
>>   (She sits up and stares at him. He goes on
>>   defiantly.)
>   I'm just being practical. Nowadays you're fit
>   for nothing unless you have an education. And you

needn't stare at me like that; any qualification
is better than nothing. You'll always get some
sort of job. Hennigan that teaches us P. T. --
that's all he has--is G. C. E. And I'm telling
you, I wouldn't give a shilling for your chances
at the moment!

MAG.

And the children?

JOE.

What children?

MAG.

Who's going to look after the dozen children when
I'm up at St. Kevin's teaching physical jerks?

JOE.

Oh, you're very smart.

MAG.

And where, may I ask, did the round dozen come
from all of a sudden?

JOE.

Cut it out, will you? You know what I meant.

MAG.

Indeed I do. And if you think I'm going to spend
my days like big Bridie Brogan----

JOE.

Who's she supposed to be?

MAG.

She's married to a second cousin once removed
of Joan O'Hara's----

JOE.

God, I might have known! If there's anyone I

hate----

MAG.

--and after her third baby the doctor told her she'd die if she had any more; but her husband was an Irish brute and she had a fourth baby----

JOE.

And she died.

MAG.

She didn't die, smartie. But she lost her sight. And then she had a fifth baby----

JOE.

And she died.

MAG.

--and she went deaf. And she couldn't walk after the sixth. And after the seventh she had to get all her teeth out----

JOE.

Sounds like the Rose of Tralee.

MAG.

And by the time she had ten----

JOE.

Her husband died laughing at her.

MAG.

She developed pernicious micropia.

JOE.

Pernicious what?

MAG.

I'm not in the habit of repeating myself. Anyhow

she's thirty-three now and----

JOE.

You made that word up.

MAG.

I did not.

JOE.

You did, Maggie.

MAG.

I did not.

JOE.

Say it again, then.

MAG.

I told you--I'm not in----

JOE.

Pernicious what?

MAG.

You're too ignorant to have heard of it. My
father came across frequent cases of it. I
don't suppose your parents ever heard of it.
(As soon as she has said this, she re-
grets it. But she cannot retract now.
Joe's banter is suddenly ended. He is
quietly furious.)

JOE.

Just what do you mean by that?

MAG.

What I say.

JOE.

I said, what do you mean by that remark?

MAG.

> You heard me.

JOE.

> You insulted my parents--deliberately.

MAG.

> I was talking about a disease.

JOE.

> You think they're nobody, don't you?

MAG.

> You were mocking me.

JOE.

> And you think your parents are somebody, don't
> you?
>> (MAG picks up a book, opens it at random,
>> turns her back to him, and begins to read.)

MAG.

> I have revision to do.

JOE.

> Well, let me tell you, madam, that my father may
> be temporarily unemployed, but he pays his bills;
> and _my_ mother may be a charwoman but she isn't
> running out to the mental hospital for treatment
> every couple of months.   And if you think the
> Brennans aren't swanky enough for you, then, by
> God, you shouldn't be in such a hurry to marry
> one of them!
>> (As soon as he has said this, he regrets it.
>> But he cannot retract now.)
> You dragged that out of me.   But it happens to be
> the truth.   And it's better that it should come out
> now than _after_ we're married. At least we know
> where we stand. . . .

(His anger is dead.)

Marg\~ret? . . . Maggie? . . .

(Stiff again.)

Well, it was you 'hat started it. And if you're going into another of your huffs, I swear to you I'm not going to be the first to speak this time.

(He picks a book, opens it at random, turns his back to her, and begins to read.)

WOMAN.

At the post-mortem on the evening of June 21 evidence of identification was given by Walter Enright. He said that the body recovered from Lough Gorm was the body of his daughter, Margaret Mary Enright.

MAN.

Michael Brennan identified the male body as that of his son, Joseph Michael Brennan.

WOMAN.

Doctor Watson said that he examined the bodies of both the deceased. There were no marks of violence on either, he said. And in his opinion-- which, he submitted, was given after a hasty examination--death in both cases was due to asphyxiation.

MAN.

Mr. Skeehan, the coroner, asked was there any evidence as to how both deceased fell into the water. Sergeant Finlay replied that there was no evidence.

WOMAN.

A verdict in accordance with the medical evidence was returned. Mr. Skeehan and Sergeant Finlay expressed their grief and the grief of the community to the parents. And it was agreed that the inquest should be held as soon as possible because the coroner took his annual vacation in the month of July.

> (JOE looks up from his book and surveys the countryside with studied intelligence. When he speaks he tries to sound as matter-of-fact as possible--as if he were continuing a conversation; but his voice is strained.)

JOE.

We're about 450 feet above sea level here; isn't that interesting?

> (Pause.)

And all that area out there was covered with fir trees once.

> (Pause.)

Willie O'Rourke did a survey of the whole area for his geography practical last term and he found out all sorts of fascinating things.

> (Pause.)

The average rainfall in Ballymore is 17.4 per cent above the national average.

> (Pause.)

That's because we get a lot of rain here.

> (Quoting.)

And the moist climate determines the type and extent of our husbandry; we are low in milk cattle and high in mountainy sheep.

> (Pause.)

And since a ring of hills cuts us off from other community centers we are traditionally inclined to be independent and self-supporting--or so he claims.

> (Pause.)

It's an interesting hypothesis.

> (Pause.)

Busy?

> (No answer. JOE continues formally.)

I'm sorry for losing my temper.
>(Opens another book.)

If you have anything to say to me, you'll find me here.
>(No answer. He looks at her.)

You crying? . . . Mag? . . .
>(Still no answer. He rises and stands behind her.)

What the hell are you crying about, Mag? . . . Mag . . .
>(He goes in front of her. She turns her back to him.)

I said I'm sorry. What more can I do? . . .
>(Pause.)

It's going to be just great if you're going to spend your life weeping all the time!
>(He casts around wretchedly for something to entertain her. Decides on mimicry. As Mrs. Moran:)

"Well, I mean to say--smoking at 'is age! I just says to 'im, 'Phil,' I says, 'if your poor daddy was alive, 'e'd be so vexed,' I says. 'Ta-ta for now, Joe. Ta-ta for now."
>(No response from MAG. As Kerrigan:)

"What about that for a bit of beef, eh? Bang. Best flat in town, lad. I could have set it a dozen times over. Bang. Bang. Bang."
>(No response.)

Mag . . . Mag, is it true that in bed at night the nuns wear their bloomers over their heads to keep them warm?
>(No response. JOE sings:)

So I gave her kisses one, kisses one;
So I gave her kisses one, kisses one;
So I gave her kisses one--now the fun has just begun
So I settled down to give her kisses more.
>(Says.)

I'd be great on TV, wouldn't I?

(No response.)

When Father Kelly sent for me last Friday fort-night, I knew I was done for, and I pretended I was so frightened I had a stammer--did I tell you that part of it?

(Pompous.)

You know, of course, Brennan, that we are going to expel you.

(Abject.)

Yes, F-f-f-father.

(Pompous.)

Because of your mother's pleading on your behalf, however, we have decided to allow you to return to sit for your examinations. But in the meantime I must insist that you remove all your belongings from the college and that you don't set foot within the grounds until the morning of the first exam-ination.

(Abject.)

T-t-t-thank you, Father.

(Pompous.)

I will not talk again about the dishonor you have brought to your school, your family, and your-self. And I trust you have made your peace with God. Good-by, Brennan.

(Abject.)

Good-by, Father.

(Pompous.)

Incidentally, Brennan, when did you develop the stammer?

(Abject.)

W-w-w-when Maggie told me she was in trouble, Father.

> (MAG began chuckling silently--and unno-ticed by JOE--at the beginning of this inter-view. Now she can contain her laughter no longer. At the last line she screams her de-light and throws herself at him, and they roll on the ground.)

MAG.

God forgive you!

JOE.

Stop! Stop! God's truth----

MAG.

God forgive you! Mocking's catching!

JOE.

Come on--quit the fooling.

MAG.

I'll give you a stammer.
(She tosses his hair and tickles him.)

JOE.

Mag--please--sorry--please--oooooh----

MAG.

I'll stammer you----

JOE.

You're hurting my----

MAG.

That'll teach you!

JOE.

You've ripped off a button----

MAG.

You're a right-looking sketch!
(Exhausted after the wrestling, they sit staring at one another. Suddenly he throws his arms around her and kisses her. As he does:)

MAN.

On Saturday, June 25, at 11:00 a. m. an inquest

was held.

WOMAN.

After various witnesses had given evidence about
the movements of the deceased on the morning of
Saturday, June 4, Doctor Watson said that the
state pathologist's report bore out his initial
opinion--that death was due to asphyxiation as a
result of drowning.

MAN.

There was no evidence as to how the deceased
got into the water. William Anthony Clerkin's
boat was perfectly sound.

WOMAN.

Sergeant Finlay stated that the temperature on
that afternoon was 77 degrees. And there was no
wind.

MAN.

An open verdict was returned.

WOMAN.

On the following Sunday, July 5, at twelve noon,
a solemn requiem mass was said by Father Kelly,
president of St. Kevin's, and a short panegyric
was preached by him. The mass was attended by
a large turnout of the townspeople and also by
pupils of Convent of Mercy and St. Kevin's.

MAN.

The bodies were buried in the local cemetery,
each in the family plot.

> (JOE and MAG are now sitting with their
> arms around one another, looking down over
> the town. The boisterousness is all over; the
> mood is calm, content, replete. MAG lights

a cigarette.)

JOE.

This day three weeks.

MAG.

Mrs. Joseph Brennan.

JOE.

As long as you're not Big Bridie Brogan.

MAG.

Who?

JOE.

The one who died of pernicious something or other.

MAG.

I made that all up.

JOE.

Thought you did.

MAG.

The flat'll be lovely and cosy at night. But you'll have to stick a bit of cardboard under the table to keep it steady. And all the junk'll have to be thrown into the spare room.

JOE.

What junk?

MAG.

Your books and things and all that.

JOE.

The slide rule cost me 37/6d. --it's staying in the kitchen. And you agreed that the dog sleeps inside.

MAG.
When do we get him?

JOE.
He's not pupped yet. I was only promised him.

MAG.
Maybe he'll be a she.

JOE.
It's a dog I'm promised--the pick of the litter.

MAG.
We'll call him . . . Austin!

JOE.
For God's sake----

MAG.
Austin's his name. Or else he sleeps out.

JOE.
Never heard of a bull-terrier called that.

MAG.
And in the daytime he can sit at the door and
guard the pram. Look----

JOE.
Where?

MAG.
The line of boarders.

JOE.
What are they up to now?

MAG.

> Going to the chapel for a visit.

JOE (counting).

> Fourteen--sixteen--eighteen--twenty----

MAG.

> It seems so remote--so long ago . . .

JOE.

> --twenty-six--twenty-eight--thirty--thirty-two----

MAG.

> And at home last week, every time I heard the
> convent bell, I cried; I felt so lost. I would
> have given anything to be part of them--to be
> in the middle of them.

JOE.

> And three nuns.

MAG.

> We were so safe . . . we had so much fun . . .

JOE.

> Mm?

MAG.

> But now I wouldn't go back for the world. I'm a
> woman at seventeen, and I wouldn't be a school-
> girl again, not for all the world.

JOE.

> I suppose I'm a man, too.

MAG.

> Would you go back?

JOE.
> Where?

MAG.
> To St. Kevin's--to being a schoolboy?

JOE.
> I never think of things like that.

MAG.
> But if you could--if you had a chance.

JOE.
> I like studying, Mag.

MAG.
> Then you'd prefer to go back.

JOE.
> No. Not there. I'm finished with all that.

MAG.
> Then you wouldn't want to go back?

JOE.
> Not to St. Kevin's. No.

MAG.
> Good.

JOE.
> Know something, Mag?

MAG.
> Mm?

JOE.
> I think I should forget about studying and London
> University and all that.

MAG.

If that's what you want.

JOE.

It's maybe not what I want. But that's the way
things have turned out. A married man with a
family has more important things to occupy his
mind besides bloody books.
(She gives him a brief squeeze. But she has
not heard what he has said. Pause.)
Ballymore.

MAG.

Home.

JOE.

See the sun glinting on the headstones beside the
chapel.

MAG.

Some day we'll be buried together.

JOE.

You're great company.

MAG.

I can't wait for the future, Joe.

JOE.

What's that supposed to mean?
(MAGGIE suddenly leaps to her feet. Her
face is animated, her movements quick
and vital, her voice ringing.)

MAG.

The past's over! And I hate this waiting time!
I want the future to happen--I want to be in it--
I want to be in it with you!

JOE.

> You've got sunstroke.
> > (She throws her belongings into her case.)

MAG.

> Come on, Joe! Let's begin the future now!
> > (Not comprehending, but infected by her
> > mood, he gets to his feet.)

JOE.

> You're nuts.

MAG.

> Where'll we go? What'll we do? Let's do some-
> thing crazy!

JOE.

> Mad as a hatter.

MAG.

> The lake! We'll dance on every island! We'll
> stay out all night and sing and shout at the moon!
> > (JOE does a wolf-howl up at the sky.)
> Come on, Joe! While the sun's still hot!

JOE.

> O mad hot sun, thou breath of summer's being!

MAG.

> Away to the furthest island.

JOE.

> We've no boat.

MAG.

> We'll take one.

JOE.

> And get arrested.

MAG.

>Coward. Then I'll take one.

JOE.

>I'll visit you in jail.

MAG.

>Quick! Quick!
>>(JOE throws his books into his bag.)

JOE.

>Hold on there.

MAG.

>Give me your hand. We'll run down the hill.

JOE.

>You'll get those pains again.

MAG.

>Your hand.

JOE.

>You're not going to run down there.

MAG.

>Come on! Come on! Come on!

JOE.

>Have sense, Mag----
>>(She catches his hand and begins to run.)

MAG.

>We're away!

JOE.

>Easy--easy----

MAG.

>Wheeeeeeeeee----

JOE.

    Aaaaaaaaah----

        (They run down the hill, hand in hand. At
        the bottom JOE takes her bicycle. Their
        voices fade slowly. Pause. Then:)

MAN.

    Beth Enright's health has improved greatly. She
    has not had a relapse for almost seven months.
    And every evening, if the weather is good, Walter
    and she go for a walk together out the length of
    Whelan's Brae.

WOMAN.

    Mick Brennan never mentions his son's name.
    After the funeral he took the tin trunk out to the
    waste ground behind Railway Terrace and burned
    all the contents. Nora Brennan has had to limit
    the amount of work she does because her varicose
    veins turned septic and Doctor Watson ordered
    her to rest. She now works afternoons only.

MAN.

    In the past eight months the population of Bally-
    more has risen from 13,527 to 13,569.

WOMAN.

    Life there goes on as usual.

MAN.

    As if nothing had ever happened.

        (The MAN and WOMAN close their texts,
        stand up, and exit, one L, one R.)

CURTAIN

Part Two

LOSERS

Scene 1

The stage is divided into three equal areas: the portion L is the back yard of a working-class terrace house; the center portion is the kitchen/
living room; the area R is the bedroom. There
should be no attempt at a realistic division of
the stage areas, no dividing walls, no detailed
furnishings; frames will indicate doors, etc.
The back yard is suggested by a dust bin and by
two high stone walls /one backstage and one R/.
It is a gray, grimy, gloomy, sunless place. The
kitchen is furnished with a table and a few chairs,
and with a disproportionately large horse-hair
black couch. The couch sits along the imaginary
wall between the kitchen and the back yard. There
are three doors leading out of the kitchen: one
to the yard, one to the scullery /unseen/ and one
to the hall/stairs /unseen/. The bedroom area is
raised on a shallow platform which is approached
by two steps /because this room is supposed to
be directly above the kitchen/. It is furnished
with a big iron double bed, a chest of drawers
with a statue of Saint Philomena on top of it /the
'altar''/ and a few chairs. Except where indicated,
the bedroom will be hidden from the audience by
a large draft screen.)

When the curtain rises, ANDY TRACEY is sitting up-
right and motionless on a kitchen chair in the
back yard. He is a man of fifty, a joiner by trade,
heavily built. He is staring fixedly through a
pair of binoculars at the gray stone wall which
is only a few yards from where he is sitting. It
becomes obvious that he is watching nothing;
there is nothing to watch, and when he becomes
aware of the audience he lowers the glasses slowly, looks at the audience, glances cautiously over

his shoulder at the kitchen to make sure that no
one in the house overhears him, and then speaks
directly and confidentially down to the audito-
rium.)

ANDY.

I'll tell you something; I see damn all through
these things. Well, I mean, there's damn all to
see in a back yard. Now and again maybe a spar-
row or something like that lands on top of the wall
there, but it's so close it's only a blur. Anyway,
most of the time I sit with my eyes closed. And
Hanna--she probably knows I do 'cause she's no
dozer; but once I come out here--I'll say that for
her--she leaves me alone. A gesture I make, and
she--you know--she respects it. Maybe because
her aul fella used to do the same thing; for that's
where I learned the dodge. As a matter of fact
these are his glasses. And this is where he was
found dead, the poor bugger, just three years
ago, slumped in a chair out here, and him all
wrapped up in his cap and his top coat and his
muffler and his woolen gloves. Wait--I'm telling
you a lie. Four years ago--aye--that's more
like it, 'cause he passed away that January Hanna
and me started going, and we won't be married
four years until next summer. Not that I knew
the man, beyond bidding him the time of day there.
Maybe he'd be inside in the kitchen there or more
likely sitting out here, and I'd say to him, "Hello there, Mr. Wilson"--you know the way, when
you're going with a woman, you try to be affable
to her aul fella--and he'd say, "Oh, hello there,
Andy" or something like that back. But you know
yourself a man that's looking through binoculars,
you don't like interrupting him. Civil wee man
he was, too. Fifty years a stoker out in the general hospital. And a funny thing--one of the male
nurses out there was telling me--all his life he
stuck to the night shift; worked all night and slept

all day, up there in that room above the kitchen.
Peculiar, eh? All his life. Never saw the wife
except maybe for a couple of hours in the evening.
Never saw Hanna, the daughter, except at the
weekends. Funny, eh? And yet by all accounts
the civilest and decentest wee man you could meet.
Funny, too. And the way things turn out in life;
when the mother-in-law found him out here about
seven o'clock that evening, she got such a bloody
fright that she collapsed and took to the bed for
good and hasn't risen since, not even the morning we got married. The heart. But that's another story. Anyway, Hanna and me, as I say, we
were only started going at the time; and then with
the aul fella dying and the aul woman taking to the
bed, like we couldn't go out to the pictures nor
dances nor nothing like any other couple; so I
started coming here every evening. And this is
where we done our courting, in there, on the
couch.

    (Chuckles briefly.)

By God, we were lively enough, too. Eh? I mean
to say, people think that when you're . . . well,
when you're over the forty mark, that you're
passified. But aul Hanna, by God, I'll say that
for her, she was keen as a terrier in those days.

    (Chuckles at the memory.)

If that couch could write a book--Shakespeare,
how are you!

    (He rises from the chair.)

Every evening, after I'd leave the workshop, I'd
go home to my own place at Riverview and wash
myself down and make a sup of tea and put on the
good suit and call in at Boyce's paper shop and
get a quarter of clove rock--that's the kind she
liked--and come on over here and there she'd be,
waiting for me, in a gray skirt and a blue jumper,
and when she'd open the door to me, honest to
God the aul legs would damn near buckle under me.

(HANNA, a woman in her late forties, comes into the
        kitchen from upstairs. She is dressed in a gray
        skirt and blue jumper. ANDY walks through the
        invisible walls, through the hall, and taps on the
        kitchen door.)

ANDY.
        Well, Hanna.

HANNA.
        Hello, Andy.

ANDY.
        Not a bad evening.

HANNA.
        There's a cold wind, though.

ANDY.
        It's sharp--sharp.

HANNA.
        But it's nice all the same.

ANDY.
        Oh, very nice--very fresh.
            (Pause.)
        Nothing startling at the factory?

HANNA.
        Not a thing. Working away.

ANDY.
        Suppose so.

HANNA.
        Cutting out shirt collars this week. And you?

ANDY.
        Still at the furniture for the new hotel. Going to

cost a fortune, yon place.

HANNA.
I'll bet you.

ANDY.
Only the very best of stuff going into it--maple
and pine and mahogany. Lovely to work with.

HANNA.
D'you see that now.

ANDY.
Lovely.
(Pause. Then ANDY produces the small bag
of sweets from his pocket.)
Here. Catch.
(He throws them to her.)

HANNA.
Oh, Andy . . .

ANDY.
They don't even ask me in the shop any more.
They just say, "Quarter pound of clove rock,
Mr. Tracey. Right you are."

HANNA.
You have me spoiled.

ANDY.
How's the mother?

HANNA (sharp).
Living. And praying.

ANDY.
Terrible sore thing, the heart, all the same.

HANNA.

> I come home from my work beat out and before
> I get a bit in my mouth she says, "Run out like
> a good child and get us a sprig of fresh flowers
> for Saint Philomena's altar."

ANDY.

> Did you go?
> > (HANNA points to the flowers wrapped in
> > paper lying on the kitchen table.)

HANNA.

> But she can wait for them.

ANDY.

> She'll miss you when you leave, Hanna.

HANNA.

> Hasn't she Cissy Cassidy next door? And if she
> hadn't a slavey like me to wait hand and foot on
> her, her heart mightn't be just as fluttery!
> > (From behind the screen comes the sound
> > of a bell--not a tinkling little bell, but a
> > huge brass bell with a long wooden handle.)
> We're early at it tonight! There's the paper.
> Have a look at it.
> > (With a bad grace she goes to answer the
> > summon. As she is about to exit:)

ANDY.

> The flowers.
> > (She grabs them, grimaces, and leaves.
> > ANDY calls after her:)
> Tell Saint Philomena I was asking for her!
> > (He chuckles at Hanna's bad humor.
> > Then he comes downstage and addresses
> > the audience.)
> The bloody bell! And nine times out of ten, you
> know, she didn't want a damn thing. Who's at the

door? Is the fire safe? Did the Angelus ring?
Is it time for the Rosary? Any excuse at all to
keep Hanna on the hop, and at the same time
making damn sure we weren't going to enjoy our-
selves. But we got cute to her. You see, every
sound down here carries straight up to her room;
and we discovered that it was the long silences
made her suspicious. That's the way with a lot
of pious aul women--they have wild dirty imagi-
nations. And as soon as there was a silence down
here, she thought we were up to something and
reached for the bloody bell. But if there was the
sound of plenty chatting down here, she seldom
bothered you. But I mean to say, if you're courting a woman there, you can't keep yapping about
the weather all night. And it was the brave Hanna
that hit on the poetry idea. Whenever we started
the courting, she made me recite the poetry--
you know there, just to make a bit of a noise. And
the only poetry I ever learned at school was a
thing called Elegy Written In a Country Church-
yard by Thomas Gray 1716-1771, if you ever heard
of it. And I used to recite that over and over
again. And Hanna she would throw an odd word
in there to make it sound natural. And by God
we'd hammer away at it until we'd stop for breath
or for a sup of tea or something; or else we'd
get carried away and forget the aul woman alto-
gether--and then the bloody bell would go and the
session would be destroyed. But they were good
times. . . . Funny thing about that poem, too;
it had thirty-two verses, and as long as I could
bull straight at it--you know, without thinking
what I was saying--I could rattle it off like a man.
But stop me in the middle of it or let me think of
what I was saying, and I had to go right back to
the beginning and start all over again. Christ,
they were rare times, too. . . .

(HANNA returns.)

ANDY.
>Well?

HANNA.
>"Is that Andrew I hear?" "No," says I, "It's
>Jack the Ripper."

ANDY.
>And how's Saint Philomena?

HANNA.
>You can laugh. "The pair of you'll be up later
>for the Rosary, won't you?"

ANDY (mock devotion).
>With the help of God.

HANNA.
>One of these days I'll do something desperate.
>>(She sits dispiritedly beside him on the
>>couch. He wants to say something ten-
>>der and consoling to her but feels he is
>>past the age for effusive, extravagant
>>language.)

ANDY.
>You're looking nice, Hanna.

HANNA.
>It's the jumper.
>>(Pause. Then he takes her hand in his and
>>strokes it. She raises his hand to her lips
>>and kisses it gently again and again. He
>>puts his arm round her shoulder. They sit
>>like this for some time.)
>We'd better keep talking.

ANDY.
    There's a nice smell of you.

HANNA.
    Soap.

ANDY.
    Nice soap.

HANNA (dreamily).
    Her bloody ear'll be twitching like a rabbit.

ANDY.
    Hanna . . .
        (Pause. They speak the next eight lines as
        if they were in a trance.)

HANNA.
    Say something, Andy.

ANDY.
    I don't want to.

HANNA.
    Please, Andy. She'll know.

ANDY.
    I don't give a damn.

HANNA.
    Andy . . .

ANDY.
    Nice . . .

HANNA.
    Please, Andy . . .

ANDY.
>Very nice . . .
>>(Very suddenly, almost violently, HANNA
>>flings herself on him so that he falls back
>>and she buries her face in his neck and kiss-
>>es and caresses him with astonishing pas-
>>sion. He is momentarily at a loss. But this
>>has happened before, many times, and he
>>knows that this is his cue to begin his poem.
>>His recitation is strained and too high and
>>too loud--like a child in school memorizing
>>meaningless facts. Throughout his recital,
>>they court feverishly.)

ANDY.
>"The Curfew tolls the knell of parting day,
>The lowing herd wind slowly o'er the lea,
>The plowman homeward plods his weary way,
>And leaves the world to darkness and to me.
>Now fades the glimmering landscape on the
>   sight----"

HANNA (to ceiling).
>It's a small world, isn't it?

ANDY.
>"Now fades the glimmering landscape on the sight.
>And all the air a solemn stillness holds,
>Save where the beetle wheels his droning flight,
>And drowsy tinklings lull the distant folds----"
>Oh, God, Hanna----

HANNA.
>Just imagine. Fancy that. Keep going, man.

ANDY.
>"Save that from yonder ivy-mantled tow'r
>The moping owl does to the moon complain
>Of such, as wand'ring near her secret bow'r,

Molest her ancient solitary reign----"

HANNA.
Andy--Andy----

ANDY.
"Beneath those rugged elms, that yew-tree's
shade----"
(HANNA groans voluptuously.)
Steady on--steady on--say something----

HANNA.
Mm?

ANDY.
She'll be listening to----

HANNA.
I don't give a damn.

ANDY (to ceiling).
Fine. Yes, indeed. Imagine that. Where in the
name of God was I?

HANNA.
"--that yew-tree's shade----"

ANDY.
What, where?

HANNA.
"Beneath those rugged elms."

ANDY.
Oh. "Beneath those rugged elms, that yew-tree's
shade,
Where heaves the turf in many a mould'ring heap,
Each in his narrow cell for ever laid,
The rude Forefathers of the hamlet sleep----"

Speak, woman!
>   (She kisses him on the mouth.)
Say something!

HANNA.
>   Kiss me.

ANDY.
>   For God's sake, woman----

HANNA.
>   Andy, kiss me.
>   (He kisses her. They forget everything.
>   The clanging of the bell shatters the si-
>   lence. HANNA breaks away roughly from
>   him, jumps to her feet, and is almost
>   trembling with fury. Her jumper and
>   skirt are twisted.)
>   Bitch! The aul bitch!

ANDY.
>   Sure you're only after leaving her! What the
>   hell can she want?

HANNA.
>   Stuffed!

ANDY.
>   Your jumper!

HANNA.
>   Agh! My . . . !
>   (She pulls the jumper right up and then
>   pulls it back into place. ANDY laughs
>   at her anger.)

ANDY.
>   Go on--go on--go on. A girl's best friend is
>   her mother.

HANNA.

Shut up, will you.

> (She adjusts her skirt and brushes back her
> hair and charges out of the room. ANDY looks
> after her and smiles contentedly. Then he
> addresses the audience.)

ANDY.

> By God, she had spunk in those days, eh? Suited
> her, too; gave her face a bit of color and made
> her eyes dance. But whatever it was that hap-
> pened to her--well, I mean to say, I think I know
> what happened . . . But, like, to see a woman
> that had plenty of spark in her at one time and
> then to see her turn before your very eyes into
> a younger version of her mother, by God it's
> strange, I'll tell you, very peculiar . . . But I
> was going to tell you about the aul woman and the
> altar and the Rosary and Saint Philomena and
> Father Peyton and all that caper. The routine
> was this. At the stroke of ten every night wee
> Cissy Cassidy--her and the aul woman's well
> met; two lisping Lizzies--she came down and
> asked Hanna and me to go up for the nightly Ro-
> sary. Fair enough. Why not? And there's the
> aul woman lying in the bed, smiling like an angel,
> and there, smiling back at her from the top of a
> chest of drawers, is this big statue of Saint Phil-
> omena. And you know, you got this feeling, with
> the flowers and the candles lit and with all the
> smirking and smiling and nodding and winking,
> you got the feeling by God that you were up to the
> neck in some sort of a deep plot or other. Like
> I knew damn well what the aul woman was up to;
> if she couldn't break it up between Hanna and me,
> at least she was going to make damn sure that I
> wasn't going to take Hanna away from her. And
> she knew that I knew what she was up to with her
> wee sermons about Father Peyton and all the

stuff about the family that prays together stays
together. And there was the pair of us, watching
and smiling, each of us knowing that the other
knew, and none of us giving away anything. By
God, it was strange. Eh? 'Cause she thought
that every time I got down on my knees in that
bedroom to join in the Rosary I was cutting my
own throat. But because I knew what she was up
to, I was safe--or at least I thought I was. She's
crafty, that aul woman. You've got to hand it to
her. By God she's crafty.

> (He goes upstage and casually lifts the news-
> paper to glance over it.)

(HANNA enters on her way through to the scullery. She
is carrying her mother's soiled tray.)

HANNA.

Look at--the invalid tray! Not a crumb on it!
Six rounds of a sliced-pan and a boiled egg! Thanks
be to God she gets no fresh air or she'd eat up the
town!

> (Knock at the front door.)

That'll be prissy Cissy.

(HANNA goes to the scullery. ANDY goes to open the
door for CISSY. She is a small, frail wisp of a
woman in her late sixties. CISSY and ANDY come
back to the kitchen briefly before CISSY goes upstairs.)

ANDY.

Hello, Cissy.

CISSY.

Good night, Andrew. You're not alone, are you?

ANDY.

Hanna's inside. How's things, Cissy?

CISSY.
>Struggling away, Andrew, thanks be to God.
>Sure as long as we have our health.

ANDY.
>That's it, Cissy.

CISSY.
>Thanks be to God, indeed. I'll go on up then,
>Andrew. . . .

ANDY.
>Right--right.

CISSY.
>You'll be up later for prayers?

ANDY.
>Aye.

CISSY.
>Thanks be to God.

(HANNA enters from the scullery. She is abrupt with
CISSY.)

CISSY.
>Hello, Hanna. How's mammy tonight?

HANNA.
>As ever.

CISSY.
>Sure that's grand.

ANDY (winking at HANNA).
>Thanks be to God.

CISSY.
>Just, Andrew--thanks be to God. Well . . . I'll

see you both at ten.

ANDY.
>Joyful mysteries tonight, Cissy, isn't it?

CISSY.
>Thursday--so it is! Oh, you're coming closer
>and closer to us, Andrew Tracey!
>>(She leaves. ANDY laughs.)

HANNA.
>Sweet wee wasp!
>>(HANNA flops down on the couch. ANDY
>>sits beside her. He sees she is in bad
>>form and tries to coax her out of it.)

ANDY.
>Tired?

HANNA.
>Done out.

ANDY.
>D'you think was Cissy ever courted?

HANNA.
>Who cares?

ANDY.
>Imagine a man putting a hand on her knee.
>"Thanks be to God, Mister."
>>(She does not laugh.)
>You're in bad aul form, Hanna.
>>(He puts his arm around her. She jumps
>>to her feet.)

HANNA.
>Not now.

ANDY.

What's wrong? Is there something the matter?

HANNA.

Sick--sick--sick--sick of the whole thing; that's
what's the matter! I can't stand it much longer!

ANDY.

Take a clove rock, Hanna.

HANNA.

What in the name of God are we going to do?

ANDY.

I've asked you half a dozen times to----

HANNA.

It's her I'm talking about! Her up there! What
do we do with her?

ANDY.

When we're married she can come with us to
Riverview. I've said that all----

HANNA.

Never! Never! The day I get married I'm get-
ting shot of her for good!
        (ANDY spreads his hands; 'What can I
        reply to that?' the gesture says.)
And no matter what you say now you know fine
well you don't want her hanging around your
neck either.

ANDY.

I hear they took old Maggie Donaldson into St.
Patrick's.

HANNA.

She's not sick enough for hospital. And they've

no spare beds for cranks.

ANDY.

> The Nazareth nuns! Let her sell this place and
> go into the Nazareth House with the money.

HANNA.

> She wouldn't go to them above all people.

ANDY.

> What else is there?

HANNA.

> I don't know, Andy. Honest to God, I just don't
> know.
>> (Pause. It dawns on ANDY that an offer is
>> expected from him. He reacts strongly to
>> the unspoken idea.)

ANDY.

> Well, damnit all, you don't expect me to come
> in here, do you? I mean to say, I have a place
> and all of my own, ready and furnished and
> everything! And leaping sky-high every time
> you hear a bloody bell isn't my idea of mar-
> ried bliss! My God, you don't expect that of
> me, do you? Well, do you?

HANNA.

> Bitch! That's what she is--an aul bitch!

ANDY.

> We're getting no younger, Hanna, you know.

HANNA.

> Tomorrow--I'll tell her tomorrow that we're
> going to clear out and she can damn well for-
> age for herself!

ANDY.

> You'll like it over at Riverview. It's--it's--(He
> sees that she is crying.)--Hanna--Hanna--aw,
> God, you're not away crying, are you----
>> (He puts his arm around her and leads her
>> to the couch. They sit. She blows her nose
>> while he tries to console her.)
> Come on, come on, there's no need for that. You
> know I can't stand seeing you crying. And you
> know I'd do anything to make you happy. We'll
> solve it some way or other. Don't you worry about
> it--we'll get some solution to it all.
>> (Very suddenly, almost violently--exactly as
>> before--HANNA flings herself on him and
>> smothers him with kisses. And as before, he
>> is taken unawares. Then he responds. But
>> after a few seconds he realizes that they are
>> being silent and he launches into his poem.)
> "The Curfew tolls the knell of parting day,
> The lowing herd wind slowly o'er the lea,
> The plowman homeward plods his weary way,
> And leaves the world to darkness and to me."
> Hanna . . . !
>> (She does not hear him. Pause. Then he
>> goes on:)
> "Now fades the glimmering landscape on the sight
> And all the air a solemn stillness holds,
> Save where the beetle wheels his droning flight,
> And drowsy tinklings lull the distant folds."
> Say something, woman!

HANNA.

> A loaf of bread costs $1/3\frac{1}{2}$ and a pound of tea 6/8.

ANDY.

> "Full many a gem of purest ray serene,
> The dark unfathom'd caves of ocean bear;
> Ev'n from the tomb the voice of Nature cries----"
> I've bucked it!

HANNA.

"Can storied urn or animated bust----"

ANDY.

What--what--what is it?

HANNA.

"Back to its mansion call the fleeting breath."

ANDY.

" . . . Call the fleeting breath,
Can Honor's voice provoke the silent dust,
Or Flatt'ry soothe the dull cold ear of death
Perhaps in this neglected spot is laid
Some heart once pregnant with celestial fire;
Hands that the rod of empire might have
    swayed. . . . "
            (But he fades out because he can no longer
            resist the barrage of her passion. Their
            mouths meet. A long kiss. Silence. Then--
            the bell. HANNA springs to her feet. This
            time ANDY is angry too.)

HANNA.

Christ!

ANDY.

For God's sake!

HANNA.

Bitch! Bitch! Bitch! Bitch! Bitch!

ANDY.

It's your fault! You make no attempt at all!

HANNA.

I don't know no poems!

ANDY.

Well . . . bloody shopping lists . . . multipli-

cation tables . . . anything!
> (Again the bell.)

What the hell can she want? Isn't Cissy with her?

HANNA (evenly).
> One of these days I'm going to strangle that wo-
> man . . . with her Rosary beads.
>> (She marches off. ANDY grabs a paper and
>> tries to read it. We now see HANNA enter
>> the bedroom and we hear Mrs. Wilson's
>> voice.)

MRS. WILSON (behind screen).
> We're going to say the Rosary a bit earlier to-
> night, dear. Cissy has a bit of a headache.

>> (HANNA removes the screen and puts it to
>> right of the set. In the large iron bed, propped
>> up against the pillows, lies MRS. WILSON.
>> Like Cissy, she is a tiny woman, with a
>> sweet, patient, invalid's smile. Her voice
>> is soft and commanding. Her silver hair is
>> drawn back from her face and tied with a blue
>> ribbon behind her head. She looks angelic.
>> CISSY, her understudy, is sitting beside her,
>> watching her with devotion. Directly facing
>> MRS. WILSON is a chest of drawers, on which
>> sits a white cloth, two candles, a large stat-
>> ue of a saint, and a vase of flowers--a min-
>> iature altar. MRS. WILSON frequently nods
>> and smiles to the statue and mouths "Thank
>> you, thank you." HANNA clumps around the
>> room, doing her chores with an ungracious
>> vigor and with obvious ill will.)

HANNA.
> Whatever suits Cissy suits me!

CISSY.
> She's looking lovely tonight, Hanna, isn't she?

It must be the good care you're taking of her.

MRS. WILSON.
I'm blessed, Cissy dear, and I know it. A good
daughter is a gift of God.
(To the statue.)
Thank you.
(To HANNA who is fixing the bed clothes
too robustly.)
That's fine, dear, thank you. Just fine.

HANNA.
Pillows.

MRS. WILSON.
What's that, dear?

HANNA.
D'you want me to beat up the pillows?

MRS. WILSON.
No, I'm grand. A wee bit of discomfort's good
for me.

CISSY.
Invalids is all saints--that's what I say.

MRS. WILSON.
Here's the matches, dear.
(HANNA goes and lights the candles.)
Cissy, could I trouble you to give Andrew a
call?

CISSY.
Pleasure. (She goes to call.)

MRS. WILSON (to HANNA).
And maybe you'd be good enough to move Saint
Philomena around a wee bit so that she's facing

me . . . just a little to the left . . . so that
we're looking at each other. . . . That's it.
Lovely. Thank you, dear.

CISSY.

Andrew!

MRS. WILSON.

God be praised a thousand times. Saint Vibiana,
Virgin and Martyr, protect us. Saint Hyacintha
de Mariscottis, look after us this day and this
night.

CISSY.

The Rosary!

ANDY.

Coming!

MRS. WILSON (to HANNA).

And my jewels, dear.

HANNA.

What are you saying?

MRS. WILSON.

Could you hand me my beads, please?
(HANNA does this.)
God bless you. Another day is nearly o'er. A
journey closer to the heavenly shore.
(CISSY returns to the bedroom.)

CISSY.

He's coming. Thanks be to God.

MRS. WILSON.

Amen to that. Poor Hanna's run off her feet,
isn't she?

CISSY.
> A labor of love.
>> (ANDY enters the bedroom. He tries to be
>> brisk and matter-of-fact in this cloying fem-
>> inine atmosphere.)

MRS. WILSON.
> Ah, Andrew!

ANDY.
> How are you tonight, Mrs. Wilson?

MRS. WILSON.
> Grand, Andrew, thanks. I have Saint Philomena
> during the day and I have you all at night.

ANDY.
> Very nice.

MRS. WILSON.
> Are you going to join us in the prayers?

HANNA.
> Didn't you send down for him!

MRS. WILSON.
> Thank you, Andrew. As Father Peyton says:
> The family that prays together stays together.

HANNA.
> Get started.

MRS WILSON.
> And Father Peyton is right, isn't he, Andrew?

ANDY.
> Right, Mrs. Wilson.

MRS. WILSON.
> If you only knew the consolation it is for me to

have you all kneeling around my bed.

CISSY.
> It's what you deserve.

MRS. WILSON.
> Thank you, Saint Philomena. Thank you.

HANNA.
> Who's giving it out?

MRS. WILSON.
> Aren't the flowers pretty, Andrew?

ANDY.
> Very nice.

MRS. WILSON.
> Hanna got them for me. But then--why wouldn't she? Didn't she take the name Philomena for her confirmation.

HANNA.
> Lookat--are we going to say the prayers or are we not?

CISSY.
> Hanna, dear, you're talking to a sick woman.
>> (MRS. WILSON lays a restraining hand on CISSY.)

MRS. WILSON.
> She's tired, Cissy. I know. I don't mind. Maybe you'd give it out tonight, Andrew, would you?

ANDY.
> I--I--I----

HANNA.
> He will not, then. I will.

(MRS. WILSON mouths her thanks to the statue. HANNA begins at top speed:)

HANNA.
In the name of the Father and of the Son and of
the Holy Ghost. We fly to thy protection, O holy
mother of God. Despise not our prayers in our
necessity, but deliver us from all dangers, O
glorious and ever blessed virgin. Thou O Lord
will open my lips.

OTHERS.
And my tongue shall announce thy praise.

HANNA.
Incline unto my aid, O God.

OTHERS.
O Lord, make haste to help me.

HANNA.
Glory be to the Father and to the Son and to the
Holy Ghost.

OTHERS.
As it was in the beginning, is now, and ever shall
be, world without end, Amen.
(They are all on their knees around the bed,
facing the altar now. While the prayers continue, ANDY gets to his feet and places the
screen in its opening position--that is com-
pletely hiding the bedroom. He then goes
behind the screen to continue the Rosary.
The lights come down slowly and the prayers
fade. Total black for about a minute.)

Scene 2

(When the lights go up ANDY is sitting as we first saw
          him, in the back yard, with his binoculars. He
          puts down the binoculars, glances cautiously ov-
          er his shoulder at the kitchen to make sure that
          no one in the house overhears him, and then speaks
          to the audience.)

ANDY.
          The big mistake I made was to come back here
          after the honeymoon--even for the couple of weeks
          that it was supposed to be at the beginning. I
          should have put the foot down then. But, like ev-
          erything happened so sudden. One bright morn-
          ing the firm turns around and says "All the sin-
          gle men in the joinery room are being sent to
          Belfast on a contract job." So there was nothing
          for it, like, but to get married. And that's what
          we done. And then when we got back from the
          three days in Dublin, there's the damn painters
          still hashing about in Riverview, and the aul wo-
          man has a bit of a flu, and Hanna's kind of wor-
          ried about her, and damnit between one thing and
          another we find ourselves back here. But it was
          to have been only for a couple of weeks--that was
          the arrangement--aw, no, there was no doubt
          about that. Two weeks, she said. And a funny
          thing, you know, looking back on it, there was
          a change in the tune even then. No, not so much
          with the aul woman--she's too crafty; Christ,
          you've got to hand it to the aul woman--but with
          Hanna. Like, you know, before we got married,
          she was full of fight. Let the aul woman step out
          of line or say something sharp to me and by God
          she jumped at her like a cock at a gooseberry.
          But somehow the spirit seemed to drain out of

her from the very beginning. Of course, when
the bloody bell would go, she would still say "The
aul bitch!" But, you know, even the way she said
it now, like kind of weary, and almost as if it
wasn't anger at the aul woman at all but more to
please me. That sort of thing. And a funny thing
about that bloody bell, too. You know, before, if
there was no noise coming from downstairs, that
ringing would be enough to waken the dead. But
after we got married, it only went when Hanna
and me started talking. Wasn't that perverse now,
eh? Oh, a deep one; deep as a well. We could
sit, by God, for a whole night and not say a word
to each other, and there wouldn't be a cheep from
upstairs. But let us start chatting and the clang-
ing would damn near shake the house. You know
there, that sort of thing.

And then there was the Rosary caper. Well, I
mean to say, a man has to draw the line some-
where. Oh, no, says I; we may have to stay together of necessity, says I, but by God it won't
be because we pray together; I'll say my own
mouthful of prayers down here. And that settled
that. I mean to say, a man has to take a stand
some time. No harm to Father U.S.A. Peyton,
says I; but all things in their proper place, and
the proper place for me and my missus is in Riverview. I'll manage rightly down here, says I,
and Father Peyton and Saint Philomena and the
three sorrowful mysteries can hammer away upstairs. She didn't like that, the aul woman, I'll
tell you. Didn't speak to me for weeks. And would
you believe what she done on me to get her own
back; it was Cissy told me with a wee toss of her
head-- "She offered you up to Saint Philomena,"
says she. Crafty? Oh, man! Hanna's thick--
there's no denying that, but she'll never have the
craft of the aul woman.

But I got her! By God I got her! . . .Or, I damn
near got her. It was this day in the works--a Fri-
day--I'll never forget it--and George Williamson
comes sidling up to me with a newspaper in his
hand and a great aul smirk on his jaw, and says
he, "So the Pope's not infallible after all, Andy, "
says he. Oh, a bad bitter Protestant, the same
Williamson. "What's that?" says I, you know
there, very quiet. "According to the paper here, "
says he, "even the Pope can make a mistake. What
d'you make of that now, eh? Isn't that a sur-
prise?" And he hands me the paper. So I pulls
out the glasses, very calm, and puts them on, and
takes the paper from him and looks at it. And
true as Christ, when I seen it, you could have
tipped me over, I was that weak. Like, for five
seconds, I couldn't even speak with excitement;
only the heart thumping like bloody hell in my
chest. For there it was in black and white before
my very eyes--THE SAINT THAT NEVER WAS.
"Official Vatican sources today announced"--I
know it by heart--"that the devotion of all Roman
Catholics to Saint Philomena must be discontinued
at once because there is little or no evidence that
such a person ever existed. " Like I never knew
I was a spiteful man until that minute; and then,
by God, my only thought was to stick that paper
down the aul woman's throat. Poor Williamson--
Christ, I shot past him like a scalded cat and out
of the workshop like the hammers of hell.

What I should have done--like, I know now--my
God, no need to tell me; instead of coopering the
thing up the way I done--but what I should have
done was wait until after the tea and then go upstairs nice and calm, you know there, and sit
down on the side of the bed very pleasant, and
say, "Have a look through the paper there, Mrs.
Wilson, " and watch, by God, watch every wee

flicker of her eye when she'd come to the big
news. . . . But I bollixed it. I know. I know. I
bollixed it. Straight from the workshop into a
pub. And when closing time comes, there I
am--blotto. And back to the house singing and
shouting like a madman.

(HANNA, who has been in the bedroom, now removes
the screen. And as she does this, ANDY goes
off. MRS. WILSON is in bed. CISSY is sitting on
the edge of the bed. HANNA has been crying for
some time and shuffles around the room, vaguely
touching different things. The candles are lit.
The atmosphere is subdued and doleful and ex-
pectant. Trite words of consolation are being
spoken. And one gets the sense of feminine sol-
idarity and of suffering womanhood.)

MRS. WILSON.
   I promise you, dear; he's all right. I know he is.

HANNA.
   But where is he?

MRS. WILSON.
   Maybe he met some of his companions.

HANNA.
   He has no companions.

MRS. WILSON.
   Maybe he's doing overtime.

HANNA.
   There's no overtime this week.

MRS. WILSON.
   Or maybe he's gone to confession.

CISSY.
    Ah! Indeed!

HANNA.
    At half-past ten? For God's sake!

MRS. WILSON.
    Well, we'll say the Rosary; that's what we'll do;
    and we'll ask God and Saint Philomena to look
    after us all. And before we're finished, you'll
    find he'll be home safe and sound to us.

CISSY.
    Thanks be to God.

MRS. WILSON.
    All down on your knees. God and his holy moth-
    er guide all our thoughts and actions this day and
    this night. In the name of the Father and of the
    Son and of the Holy Ghost. The five sorrowful
    mysteries of the most holy Rosary----
        (Remote sounds of ANDY singing.)

HANNA.
    Sshhh!

MRS. WILSON.
    The first sorrowful mystery--the agony in the
    garden----

HANNA.
    Sh! Sh! Listen! Listen!

(The women freeze. Downstairs ANDY staggers into
    the kitchen, singing "God Save Ireland." The
    women are horrified.)

MRS. WILSON.
    Is it----?

HANNA.
>Shut up!

CISSY.
>Singing! Andrew?

MRS. WILSON.
>He's not----?

HANNA.
>He is!

CISSY.
>A drunk man!
>>(ANDY flings his coat on the couch and reels
>>to the the bottom of the stairs. Calls up:)

ANDY.
>Mrs. Wilson! Hello there, old mammy Wilson!
>I've got news for you . . . big, big news.
>>(HANNA is terrified. MRS. WILSON takes
>>control.)

HANNA.
>What in the name of God----?

MRS. WILSON.
>Leave him to me.

ANDY.
>Stay where you are till I come up . . . very im-
>portant, old mammy . . . very important . . .

MRS. WILSON.
>Don't say a word. Leave everything to me.

CISSY.
>Drunk--the dirty animal!

MRS. WILSON.
    Quiet.

HANNA.
    But what if he----

MRS. WILSON.
    Don't worry. I'll settle him. And stop whining!
        (ANDY enters and surveys the three alarmed
        faces. He has the newspaper in his hand.)

ANDY.
    By God, if it's not the Dolly Sisters!
        (He gives them a grand bow.)
    And Saint Philomena!
        (Grand bow to the statue.)
    All we need now is Father Peyton . . . Where's
    Father Peyton? . . . I'll tell you something;
    The family that drinks together sinks together.

MRS. WILSON.
    Andrew!

ANDY.
    "The cock's shrill clarion, or the echoing horn----"

CISSY.
    Dirty animal!

ANDY.
    "No more shall rouse them from their lowly bed.
    For them no more the blazing hearth shall burn,
    Or busy housewife ply her evening care----"
    Thomas Gray, 1716-1771.

HANNA.
    Mother, please!

MRS. WILSON.
Listen to me, Andrew!

ANDY.
She (Hanna) knows what I'm talking about 'cause she's my wife----

MRS. WILSON.
If you don't behave yourself----

ANDY.
As for prissy Cissy here----

CISSY.
All for Thee, all for Thee----

ANDY.
You'll go down with the white bobbins. Know what that means, prissy Cissy? The white bobbins? It means you'll never know your ass from your elbow.

HANNA.
Andy!

MRS. WILSON.
I'll give you one minute to get out of this house!

ANDY.
News for you, old mammy--here, in this paper.
(To the statue.)
And news for you, darling, too.

MRS. WILSON.
Get out!

ANDY (to statue).
You've been sacked.

MRS. WILSON.
> I said get out!

ANDY (to statue).
> You and me--both sacked.
>> (He comes over to the bed with the paper.)

HANNA.
> Stop it, Andrew! Stop it!

ANDY.
> In black and white. . . . Read it. . . . It says,
> we don't stay together--that's what it says. Fath-
> er Peyton, it says, you're head's a marley.
> That's what it says.

CISSY.
> Dirty, dirty animal.

MRS. WILSON.
> I warned you! I gave you ample warning! And
> if you think you can profane in this room----
>> (She breaks off and clutches her heart and
>> cries out.)

CISSY.
> What--what is it?

HANNA.
> Mother! Mother?
>> (ANDY staggers back to the altar. On his
>> way he kicks over the bell. He laughs.)

ANDY.
> "The curfew tolls no more the knell of parting day."
>> (He lifts the statue and waltzes with it.)
> Come on, darling; we know when we're not wanted.

MRS. WILSON.
>Don't--touch--that----

CISSY.
>The statue!

HANNA.
>Andrew!

CISSY.
>Oh, my God!

MRS. WILSON.
>Stop him! Stop him!
>>(Chaos and confusion as HANNA and CISSY rush at ANDY and wrest the statue from him. Everyone is shouting at the same time. MRS. WILSON gets out of bed and CISSY puts a coat around her.)

CISSY.
>Come on! Come on! Into my place!

HANNA.
>Are you all right, Mother?

ANDY.
>"Large was his bounty and his soul sincere,
>Heav'n did a recompense as largely send----"

MRS. WILSON.
>Take all--statue--candles--cloth----

CISSY.
>Brute animal!

MRS. WILSON.
>Oh, my heart----

HANNA.

>Out--quick!

>>(CISSY and HANNA each take an arm of MRS.
WILSON and they support her out. HANNA
also takes the altar things. MRS. WILSON
groans loudly and pathetically. CISSY con-
soles her. ANDY reels over to the bed and
sits on it. He is muttering to himself. HAN-
NA leaves the others, goes to him, and sticks
her face into his, and hisses:)

>You'll regret this day, Andrew Tracey! You'll
regret this day as long as you live!

>>(She then pulls over the screen and joins
CISSY and her mother who go off chattering
hysterically. ANDY rises and watches them
go. He shouts after them:)

ANDY.

>We're sacked, Philomena -- both of us -- both
sacked--what the hell are we going to do now--
eh? What the hell are we going to do now?

>>(He goes downstairs and disappears.)

Scene 3

>(After a few seconds he reappears--sober, in cardigan
and house slippers--in the kitchen and goes out
to the yard where he sits on the seat and looks
through the binoculars. Puts them aside, glances
over his shoulder as usual, and then addresses
the audience.)

ANDY.

>I don't think I told you about the tenant I have over
in Riverview. Retired accountant. Quiet couple.
No kids. He pays me on the first Saturday of every month. Sometimes if the weather's good I

take an odd walk over there and look at the out-
side of the house. He has rose trees in the front
and vegetables at the back. Very nice. Very
cozy. But by the time you get home from work and
get washed you don't feel like going out much. So
I usually sleep at the fire for a while and then
come out here for a breath of air. Kills an hour
or two. And then when the bell rings I go up to
the aul woman's room for prayers. Well, I mean
to say, anything for a quiet life. Hanna sleeps
there now, as a matter of fact, just in case the
aul woman should get an attack during the night.
Not that that's likely. The doctor says she'll go
on forever.

And a funny thing, you know, nothing much has
changed up there. Philomena's gone, of course.
But she still has the altar and she still lights the
candles and has the flowers in the middle and she
still faces it when she's praying and mouths away
to it. I says to Cissy one night I says, "Who's
she supposed to be praying to?" "A saint, " says
she very quick. "What saint?" says I, "Sure
there's no statue there." "I'm not blind, " says
she. "Well, I mean to say, " says I, "what does
she think she's at?" "True enough, there's no
statue there, " says Cissy, "but we have a saint
in our mind when we're praying even though we
have no figure for it. " "What saint?" says I.
"Aha!" says she, "That's something you'll never
know! Wild horses wouldn't drag that out of us.
You robbed her of Saint Philomena but you'll never be told who it is!"

Crafty, eh? And when I go into the bedroom she
smiles and nods at me and you can see her lips
saying "Thank you thank you, " to the altar. And
when we kneel down, she says, "It's so nice for

me to have you all gathered around my bed. As
a certain American cleric says, "The family
that prays together stays together."

By God, you've got to admire the aul bitch. She
could handle a regiment.
    (He lifts the binoculars, puts them in front
    of his eyes, and stares at the wall in front
    of him. The lights go down slowly until the
    stage is totally black.)

THE END

WINNERS

MAN and WOMAN: The commentators are in their late fifties and are carefully dressed in good dark clothes.

MAG: Mag is seventeen and though not really beautiful, her vivacity gives her a distinct attraction. She is inclined to be extreme in her enthusiasms. Whatever she likes, she loves; whatever she dislikes, she hates--momentarily. She is either very elated or very depressed, but no emotion is very permanent. She wears a blue school blazer, white blouse and gray skirt.

JOE: Joe is seventeen and a half. He is at the age when he is earnest about life; and he has a total and touching belief in the value and importance of education. He is dressed casually in school clothes.

LOSERS

ANDY: He is a man of fifty, a joiner by trade, heavily built. His work mates look on him as a solid, decent, reliable, slightly dull man. Because his mind is simple, direct, unsubtle, he is unaware of the humor of the things he says. He wears ordinary work clothes throughout the play, carrying a coat in Scene 2, and adding a cardigan and house slippers in Scene 3.

HANNA: Hanna is in her late forties. She works in a local shirt factory, lives alone with her invalided mother, and until Andy came on the scene had not been out with a man for over twenty years. This sudden injection of romance into a life that

116

seemed rigidly and permanently patterned has transformed a very plain spinster into an almost attractive woman. With Andy she is warm; with her mother she reverts to waspishness. Because neither Andy nor Hanna is young there is a curious diffidence between them. And yet when they begin courting, it is Hanna who takes the initiative and caresses him with a vigor and concentration that almost embarrasses him. She is dressed in a gray skirt and blue jumper.

CISSY: She is a small, frail woman in her late sixties. She lives next door, is a daily visitor and because of the close friendship between herself and Mrs. Wilson she has a proprietary air in the house. A lifetime spent lisping pious platitudes has robbed them of all meaning. The sickly piousity she exudes is patently false. She wears a simple, plain dress appropriate to an older woman.

MRS. WILSON: Hanna's mother is a tiny woman with a sweet, patient invalid's smile. Her voice is soft, but commanding. She wears night clothes and her silver hair is drawn back from her face and tied with a blue ribbon behind her head. She looks angelic.

WINNERS

GENERAL: Two high-backed chairs; large pentagonal platform approached by four or five stairs.

MAN and WOMAN: Bound manuscripts.

MAG: Bicycle; attache case containing schoolbooks, sandwiches wrapped in paper, paper cups, an apple etc.; cigarettes and matches.

JOE: Leather satchel containing schoolbooks, dictionary, papers, handkerchief, pen knife.

LOSERS

GENERAL: Dustbin; two high stone walls; table; chairs; large black horsehair couch; three doors; platform for bedroom area approached by two steps; large iron double bed with bed clothes and pillows; chest of drawers on which sits a white cloth, two candles, a large statue of Saint Philomena, and a vase of flowers--a miniature altar; large draft screen. Scene 1 - Flowers wrapped in paper on kitchen table, newspaper on table, coat in bedroom.

ANDY: Pair of binoculars; small bag of clove rock sweets; newspaper.

HANNA: Tray with dirty dishes on it; handkerchief.

MRS. WILSON: Large brass bell with long wooden handle; matches; Rosary beads.

118